Intelligent Investors

How top fund managers think about investing our money

Lawrence Gosling
with Jane Wallace

CentralBooks

Contents

Introduction

When *Investment Week* magazine was first published on 30th January 1995 it was with a very simple mission – to provide an opportunity for our readers – professional financial advisers and wealth managers – to hear the views of those people who managed their clients' money – fund managers.

It was a simple objective because historically fund managers had not had a dedicated platform to share their views, despite their importance to literally millions of savers, policyholders, pension scheme members and retirees.

In 2015 these fund managers manage or invest in excess of £5.5 trillion for investors but hardly anyone outside financial services can name a fund manager in the UK (unlike America where millions of ordinary people know who Warren Buffett is).

I hope this book changes that to a small extent and gives readers a window into the brilliant minds of just a handful of those entrusted with looking after the nation's long-term savings.

Many of those interviewed I have been lucky to know for longer than the 20 years the magazine has been in existence and they have been selected with no greater logic than I have always found them interesting and fascinating people to talk to. There were many more I would have liked to interview, but time and space were limited.

All those interviewed were very generous in sharing their insights and opinions, and I thank them for doing so. It is true to say they share a common belief that the more investors –

private or professional – understand how they think, then better investment decisions will be made.

A number of the interviews are in a question and answer format because it allows the fund managers' words to hopefully come across in the truest sense of their meaning – but also I'm intrinsically lazy so it was quicker for me to edit the chapters!

My colleague Jane Wallace volunteered half-way through the project to take on some interviews, so there is a difference of styles which I hope makes for a varied read.

I'd like to thank fellow journalist, Scott Longley, for ploughing through all the interviews and bringing some order to much of the writing, particularly my verbose questions, and I'd like to thank Jay Young for transcribing hours of interviews and adding some helpful comments.

Lastly I'd like to thank Nick Train of Lindsell Train who inspired the whole idea when talking at a seminar for professional investors about what his investment inspirations had been, and then spending another few hours expanding on his ideas.

This book is published to coincide with the 20th year of *Investment Week* and all the proceeds go to two children's charities – Place2Be and CHICKS – both of which are investing in the future of young people in the UK.

And lastly I'd like to thank my wife Debbie, my children Emily, Katherine and Chris, and granddaughter Faith – who will always be the best investment I'll ever make.

Lawrence Gosling, founding editor of *Investment Week*

Chapter 1

The Engineer Fascinated by Financial Markets

Anne Richards interviewed by Jane Wallace

From particle physics colliders to the world of fund management might seem like something of a leap, but for Anne Richards, having studied electrical engineering it was the opening up of the world of investment that she found exciting. With an element of humour, she says that she enjoys the job of overseeing the work of the fund managers at Aberdeen Asset Management. "You can't manage fund managers," she says. "You sort of herd them gently."

Jane Wallace: You started off as an engineer. What attracted you to fund management?

Anne Richards: I was working on the predecessor for the Large Hadron Collider at CERN. We were building a lepton collider and I worked on the control system for a bit of kit which kept the beams apart and then brought them into collision when they reached the right energy level.

It was very exciting and you would pass Nobel prize-winners going up and down the corridor. But I gradually realised that there was a very long time horizon involved. Once I asked a colleague how long he thought it would take us to find what we were looking for. He said, in all seriousness, about 30 years, which was pretty spot on actually. And I remember thinking that, in 30 years' time, I would be 52 and, blimey, that sounded very, very old. Although it doesn't sound quite so old now.

I realised then that I didn't have the focus on one single driving mission which most people who I was working with had. I decided not to stay at CERN and I came back to the UK to work for a firm of technology consultants. I knew nothing about how to read a P&L so I did a certified diploma in accounting and finance at night-school, which was my first introduction to anything business-related. I didn't find it boring, it seemed quite interesting. But I wasn't really enjoying Cambridge: it is very flat and I like mountains. So I thought, I really have to go back to Europe. And somebody said, why don't you join INSEAD? Which I did, this time with a husband in tow, because we'd just got married. There I did a course in financial markets and it was the first time I had ever opened a Financial Times or looked at a screen with prices on it.

And I just fell in love with it because it was constantly changing. The information flow is continuous. Every morning you wake up, you open your eyes and whoosh, there's a new picture in front of you! I found that so stimulating. The physics world is incredible. I love it and have huge respect for it, but the immediacy of constantly pitting yourself against the market I always found incredibly fascinating.

JW: So you became a fund manager?

AR: I started as an engineering analyst. Fortunately nobody actually let me do any of the buying and selling at that stage. But I did quite quickly realise that I wanted to manage the portfolio.

Then I moved to JPMorgan as a portfolio manager where I stayed for five years until I was headhunted to go into Mercury Asset Management and its Alpha team.

I really enjoyed it and I worked with some fantastic people but being a subsidiary of a much larger firm brings its own challenges. For example, you might get asked to do cost-cutting which is relevant to the mother ship but not to your own business unit. So I began to think I wanted to work for an independent. Then the opportunity came up at Edinburgh Fund Managers. It was a seat on the board and I would be chief investment officer (CIO). I would have a much smaller business, but it would be mine to control.

That proved an interesting period because it was in 2002. This was not quite when the market bottomed but we were beginning to feel we were in a bit of trouble. Then during my gardening leave, EFM lost its single biggest client so I knew that it was going to be a bit of a challenge.

Unfortunately, I hadn't picked up on the fact that the chief executive had fallen out with his major shareholder in a really big way. Within six weeks of joining, we were presented with a letter from 50% of the shareholders requisitioning an EGM to remove the chief executive and the four non-executive directors.

So we called an emergency board meeting and the chairman decided to resign, even though the shareholders hadn't requested his resignation. He then encouraged all of the other non-executive directors to resign, which left the chief executive, myself, and the chief operating officer as the only remaining board members. We had another board meeting at which myself and the COO had to ask the chief executive to leave. That was quite squeaky. We started the day with seven or eight board members and we ended the day with two.

Then it all got worse because this was around November 2002 when the market was tanking. Because we'd lost this major client, we had to put in place fairly draconian measures to make sure that we could keep paying the bills. There we were, two young, very inexperienced executives who had ended up running a business with 250 people and all sorts of challenges.

Eventually we got two really fantastic non-executive directors, who were really committed to helping us, and we put the business up for sale. Aberdeen approached us with a really clever deal which would help recapitalise Aberdeen as well solve EFM's problems. We've kept many, many of the clients that came across at that time and it really was the start of Aberdeen on its road to recovery.

JW: Has that been your biggest challenge so far in your career?

AR: Probably, because it was a crisis point in markets as well as a crisis point in the business. But I wouldn't underplay 2008. When Lehman went, nobody really knew where the dominos were going to fall and what the consequences might be. We hadn't really been in a situation like this before where counterparty risk on a major scale was something you had to worry about.

Before the Fed stepped in in March 2009, we had some funds with leverage. We also had funds with redemptions on them at a time when you couldn't get a price on some of the bonds. And we knew the bonds were good quality; that they would repay on maturity. But nobody was willing to take the risk of putting the capital up. So we were in a situation when, if you got a redemption, you had to work out how to fund it at a fair price as opposed to a realistically deliverable price. We were never quite sure from what angle something else could hit the markets. But we never sat around wondering if the business would survive so I think EFM in 2002 was a bigger challenge.

JW: Is the role of CIO merely managing the fund managers?

AR: There's quite a big part of the role now which is around the governance of investment. For example, I chair the investment committee which looks at any new products that we want to launch.

Another part concerns our funds – hundreds and hundreds of them across the business. We have to review their performance, we have to review the risk that's taken on those funds and we have to test whether that is compatible with what clients expect from us. Then we have to identify when a portfolio is performing in a way differently to how we would

5

expect. If you look back, the regulatory-driven aspect of what you do as the CIO has changed enormously. It's a much, much bigger part of my job.

Then there's a bit around markets. I'm really lucky because I get to hear what our high-yield guys in the States are saying, or what our pan-European equity team is thinking. Then I try to construct a coherent narrative around it in terms of "what is this telling us when you put it all together?" That's the really interesting part of my job.

I do get the joy of talking to lots of fund managers. You can't manage fund managers. You sort of herd them gently, with cans of Felix that you put down on the ground and try to encourage them in the right direction. So there's a bit of that. For the most part though, our guys are quite sensible and they're nice people. They have their idiosyncrasies but we don't have some of the egos that you see in other parts of the City.

There's some client-facing work too such as meeting investors and talking to them about world events. As I'm also a director of the plc, I spend some time with shareholders. And then we've got a business that we try and run in between all of the above.

So I have a really varied role and I can put my nose into any part of the business that I think looks interesting. So I get to talk about technology and strategy, as well as thinking about graduate recruitment.

JW: On that point, can you explain about your work in encouraging girls to study STEM (science, technology, engineering and maths) subjects?

AR: Over the years I've become increasingly convinced of the business case for diversity and inclusion. For many years, I assumed that we lived in an entirely equal and fair world because we had legislative equality. Therefore, like many of my generation, I thought that that was sufficient. Now, of course, I've realised that it's not. There's still a lot of societal bias and it has real consequences.

JW: What do you mean by societal bias?

AR: Bias is at so many different levels. So let's take it away from gender, as an example. Just under 15% of the American male population is a height of six feet or above. But the proportion of chief executives of Fortune 500 companies who are six feet tall or more is 58%. So when we talk about societal bias, we see tall people and we think "leader". That helps them progress through organisations.

My take on this is we all have these unconscious biases. Our unconscious processes vast reams of data, far more than our conscious mind does. That's good because otherwise none of us would be able to cross the road. But I think we have to understand that we've got these biases and start thinking about what we need to do to adjust for them.

It matters because a mixed team – and the more jumbled up the better – will explore a problem from more angles and is more likely to find a good solution. And often a solution that nobody else has thought of.

The evidence for that in multiple different situations is huge and yet it's something that tends not to be made a management objective. We allow the societal biases, we all observe and absorb them, and yet we don't recognise there's a business imperative to adjust for them, not because of a fairness argument but because of a business advantage argument.

I have a particular passion for women in STEM because, if you look at the data, we seem to be going backwards there in some respects. Biases are being imposed, particularly in Western societies, at a really early age. There's some shocking stuff like if you give boys and girls a maths test, they will do broadly equally well at it, unless you ask them to write down at the top of the page whether they are a boy or a girl. This causes the girls' performances to degrade by about 10% because you're putting in that trigger, "Oh, I'm a girl, I'm doing maths".

Deep-rooted biases are a problem because we have a massive shortage of technically literate people across the UK. We know that 80% plus of jobs in the future will require some level of digital skills and yet, in this country, just over half of schools don't put a single girl forward for A-level physics, for example.

These are quite staggering numbers and we're worse than many other countries in this respect. We are in fact restricting the overall economic growth of the country because we are conditioning girls not to go into STEM areas and denying them the opportunity to discover they actually like the subject matter.

JW: Who is doing the conditioning?

AR: There's no one single answer but we are all watching far more on the screen. When you look at the images that come through TV and film, you see a very small proportion, smaller than in the real world, of female scientists or female engineers or even working mums. Women are much more often portrayed as victims or in stereotypical care roles. So again, we're conditioning both the women and the men that this is how you should think of yourself as a woman and these are the roles you do.

I'm not say people are evil or wicked and doing this with intent. But we have to have an awareness that this is happening and try to make adjustments.

JW: As a female working in two stereotypically male careers – engineering and fund management – were you ever discouraged? How did you deal with that?

AR: My parents both came from underprivileged backgrounds and had to fight incredibly hard to get a university degree. As children, we never didn't have a working mum: we always had two parents out at work the whole time. There was never any hint or suggestion, as two girls and a boy, that we were anything other than equal. We were all pretty much left to our own devices and nobody ever said: "Do your homework!" If you didn't do your homework, that was your problem, it wasn't their problem. They just said, "Well if you don't do it, you're stupid". So that was the environment I grew up in. Self-sufficiency; be independent; don't get into debt – that was the mantra.

It really helped in investment management because I was oblivious to some of the sensitivities you mention. Everything I'd done had been pushing and pushing. At CERN, I was the youngest by some margin. My engineering group was 49 blokes, me and Bernadette, our lovely secretary. So I was used to always being a bit different. You become immune to it, actually.

I don't walk into a room and think "I'm female". Unless somebody does something which demonstrates to me that I'm being treated differently because of it, I tend to coast through and ignore most of the rubbish. I think I was lucky to inherit my parents' attitude.

JW: Some women haven't been so lucky. Should there be more regulation to help them?

AR: I think more data transparency would help. The more transparent we can get the data, the more businesses and organisations will be aware of where the challenges in their own organisations lie. I applaud the efforts that have already been made to create more transparency around pay and performance but there's a lot more we could do.

It's quite easy to put in a quota at a non-exec level and tick that box. It's much tougher to put in a quota in the management pipeline and channel. I wouldn't say it's impossible but the risk of unintended consequences is really big. Before we get to that point of saying we absolutely have to do that in order to make progress, we need to raise awareness that organisations and businesses should actively seek out diversity because it will be to their greater credit. They will advance more; they will get a better outcome for the business as a whole. It's about making the pie bigger.

JW: Let's talk about investment management. What factors make a company attractive to you?

AR: Like everything in life, you learn over time. There is an evolution between what attracts you when you jump into the market aged twenty-something and then what you think is a sensible approach at forty-something.

Today the first starting point is a healthy scepticism. If anything sounds too good to be true, it almost certainly is. There will be one chance in 10,000 that it's not and you get the occasional Apple – the truly mind-blowing, mind-expanding opportunity. But those are the exceptions.

For sure, you should try to identify those opportunities but the core of your investment thesis should be much more boring. It's about understanding the assets you're buying when you invest in the company, their quality and the cash flow they generate. Cash is a much harder thing to hide and obfuscate than profit. Profit is a very, very subjective number; cash is still subjective, but it's not as subjective as profit.

Understanding physical assets, the cash that comes off those assets and who is looking after whose interests in the business is really important. Where is the management incentive? Where are their interests aligned with yours?

Because if they're not aligned with yours then as a minority shareholder, which you always are when you come in as an investor, you will end up on the wrong side of that trade sooner or later.

Trading portfolios is fun and exciting but nothing beats hard work and doing the boring stuff really well. I think that's a real lesson for people and we're not good at getting that message out. This isn't about glitz and trading rooms and Wall Street films that show people shouting at each other. That's not what our business is about.

It is about identifying which businesses are going to grow over time, steadily. Are people going to buy more soap powder? Are people going to need more copper? If we go to driverless cars, what will happen to the insurance market? Those are sensible questions to ask.

JW: So what about risk then? How did you handle risk in your own portfolios? And do you have a better understanding of risk after 20 years in the business?

AR: The evolution of risk is very interesting. What is risk? It's a very basic question. It's really about the possibility of loss of value: not just financial risk, it could be reputational risk. There are all sorts of ways to think about risk. In the investment world, you're really talking about the risk of permanent loss of capital – volatility of capital. Unless you have a particular drawdown need, it's not necessarily something you should be worried about.

When I came into the City, in 1992, the world was moving to the concept of tracking error, which is really the standard deviation of return away from a benchmark return. The concept of value at risk (VAR) came into the lexicon for the first time and we started looking at statistics as a shorthand proxy for risk.

That concept has an appeal to me. I like maths, I do maths – I get that. But over 20 years, it's become increasingly obvious that, because VAR is such a narrow definition, it's become downright misleading and, at times, actually dangerous.

In 2008, one of the reasons we got into difficulty was because everyone was using the same VAR models. And the problem with VAR is that if it says something is a one in 200 event, or a one in 500 event, there's a risk that people say "it's very unlikely, therefore we don't need to worry about it". However, in the year it happens, it doesn't matter that it's not going to happen for another 199 years. When it happens, you need to have the cash there to get you through.

I think that's what we missed in those interpretations of risk. Over time, we've moved beyond the simplistic view that either short-term volatility or a statistical representation can in any way encapsulate the entirety of risk. It can't. So that's been a big shift.

Now when I think about risk, I'll frame it in terms of scenarios. I won't try to identify the probability of a nasty event happening and then do a weighted average of the outcomes. I'll ask, if this event happens, what is the impact and could we cope? If the answer is no, then we need to think about making adjustments so we get to a situation where we can.

I've no easy answers on risk, apart from diversification. You won't necessarily avoid losing money, but if you've built in different scenarios and asset classes that might behave differently in those different scenarios, hopefully you won't lose money everywhere.

We definitely have a void in the world of portfolio theory. We don't really have anything today which allows us to encompass the totality of horizon risk, of sequencing risk, of counterparty risk, of liquidity risk, of central bank risk – all of these things. The economic backdrop isn't too bad and we are seeing growth in most parts of the globe. But this is a new world in terms of central bank action. We have no rule book for how they're going to unwind what they've been winding up over the last six or seven years.

JW: Can we build a new model to address that void?

AR: I don't think it's a quantitative model. I think the answer is more likely to be in the behavioural sciences than in the purely quantitative world. I think data science will start giving us some answers on this.

JW: How would that work?

AR: By data science, I mean big data, or the ability to aggregate masses of data. Then you can see trends and patterns which are not evident at the micro level. I saw this

14

fascinating snippet on TV in America which reported on how somebody had analysed data from satellites on supermarket car parks, such as how many cars drive in and out, at what times and so on, all across the country. The individual number plates can't be read, obviously, but you can analyse the trends in this data and work out from it which supermarkets are trading well, which are trading less well, and in what periods – that's really powerful.

This is big data in action. When you put all of the car movements together, you can actually start to drive correlations and even more important, causality. It's a competitive advantage for supermarkets because it can tell them not just how they're trading but how their competitors are faring as well.

So what does that mean for financial markets? I don't know the answer to that yet but we are starting to be able to answer different questions because of this ability to aggregate data differently. And if we can start to see exchange data or portfolio turnover data aggregated in different ways, or if we can start to see how people's behaviour, in terms of when they're buying, say, on Amazon, or the Google searches that they're doing, is related to their feeling of financial prosperity or the economic cycle, maybe that will give us new ways of thinking about managing risk.

This is why I say I don't think in ten years' time we will be looking at risk models which are purely statistically driven. We'll be looking at things which are much more holistic than that, which incorporate some of the behavioural trends.

INVESTOR TIPS

Data from the US investment industry shows that the single biggest destructor of value is that investors buy when the market has gone up and they sell after a collapse, says Richards.

Starting to save early in life and continuing to put away money regularly is a starting point for financial success, she argues. But key to preserving the value of savings is circumventing the human bias to buy high and sell low.

She says: "If you are tempted to buy something which has gone up an awful lot, probably don't. And if you are tempted to sell something that has gone down quite a lot, it might still be the right thing to do, but just stop and check."

Financial prudence is another quality towards which Richards feels investors should aspire. She pointed out that her upbringing, by parents who took a dim view of debt and paid off any necessary borrowing such as a mortgage as quickly as possible, has encouraged this slant. However, while she acknowledged that leverage can lead to increased gains, being debt-free brings its own rewards.

"You have a real freedom if you are financially prudent that you don't have if you're worried about where the next pay check is coming from to meet the payment to the bank," she says. "That's reassuring when you work so close to the financial markets which can go wrong at any time and you can be easily out of a job."

Richards also advises keeping the workplace in

perspective. She attributed this ability in herself to the experiences of her sister and mother who have both worked as teachers in very underprivileged areas.

"We do live in a bubble here," she says. "But however tortuous and difficult things get at work, I've never had any difficulty about shrugging my shoulders and thinking, well the world's not ended, nobody died. We can get all chewed up about work and actually sometimes you have to walk away and give yourself space."

Her final piece of advice is not to make knee-jerk decisions late in the week.

"They usually go wrong, so avoid doing anything critical on a Friday afternoon," she says.

Chapter 2

Britain's Benjamin Graham?

Nick Train interviewed by Lawrence Gosling

Co-founder of Lindsell Train, Nick Train now manages the company's UK equity portfolios and jointly manages the global funds alongside the Lindsell Train Investment Trust. Before founding his firm with Michael Lindsell in 2000, Train was head of global equities at M&G Investment Management and previous to that he spent 17 years at GT Management. Lindsell Train was founded on the principle that all that counted was absolute returns, and he sticks by the Buffett-like principles of investing in great businesses – and holding on to them.

Lawrence Gosling: "If you want different performance, you must invest differently."

That was Sir John Templeton. What does that mean to you and how have you tried to implement that over the course of your investing career?

Nick Train: To me, there are two aspects to that quote. I am not sure what the order of significance is but the first is that I think it is well acknowledged that some parts of my industry perhaps do their clients a disservice by, to put it crudely, charging a high fee for actually delivering a product that is not very different from the shape of the benchmark or from what other big players in the market are doing. In a world where technology has made the provision of both indexed funds and ETFs much more readily available to many more investors, very cheaply, I really feel that those of us who claim that we are active managers, who are trying to achieve a superior return to justify charging that fee, it really behoves us to be doing something different. Because if we are not doing something different from the average, or from the benchmarks, really clients ought to be told that they can go and buy an ETF. So that's one aspect of that Templeton quote.

The other is that for understandable psychological reasons – which are very difficult even for me to fight against – there is a great sense of safety in numbers in financial markets. Financial markets are scary, they are volatile, and it is much more comfortable to be doing something that you know lots of other people are doing, because it limits your exposure, the risks you are taking. The price that investors pay for that tendency for people to gather together in herds, again, is this mediocrity of performance.

I was lucky enough to actually hear Sir John giving a speech – he had a list of 10 or 12 observations to make. As a young investment manager, that one was the one that really struck me most forcibly; that you are a young guy or a young woman in this industry, and as an investor, you want to make a mark. OK. But there is a price you have to pay to achieve that, and that is you have got to take the risk of doing something differently because otherwise you are not going to get anywhere.

LG: How do you balance that risk of doing something different from just being wilfully contrarian?

NT: I am not sure. To be candid I think back to the very early stages of my career, when I was first given responsibility for other people's precious capital, and I think now what were my employers thinking of? How naive was I? How much was I feeling my way forward, experimenting with other people's money to try and develop a style? But on the other hand, it is hard to think of any other way that someone can develop those skills. I would hope that young professional investors would be given a chance to develop their own style and to express themselves. But I would say to anybody who is thinking about allocating their precious savings, be careful about giving too much of it to young people who do not have the experience. I do not know the way to resolve it. But in the end in order to make progress you have to take responsibility for the decisions and for the outcomes.

LG: From those early days, do you remember any investment decisions where you felt you really learnt some lessons?

NT: Almost too many. I will have made every mistake. You look at an extraordinary career like Neil Woodford's. Long may it continue by the way, and I am being slightly unfair to Neil, but I would guess there are no more than half a dozen really critical strategic decisions that he has taken in a long, long career, and those six decisions have been the ones that have been the difference between him being justifiably a contemporary hero in this industry, and a nobody. Relatively few major strategic judgements make such a difference.

What I remember from the earlier phase of my career was taking a Buffett idea that just had a transformative effect on both my performance, hence my reputation, but also my confidence in doing what I was doing. It was in the late '80s, early 1990s and I built a really major exposure for the fund I was running then to the regional ITV companies; you will remember these things, perhaps not many of your readers will, Thames, Yorkshire, Carlton, Anglia TV. I owned them all in big size and that was, from a Templeton point of view, a really contrarian thing to do. It really was.

But it also borrowed directly from the example of Berkshire Hathaway; Buffett had very, very successful investments in US TV companies and, as he always does, had written so transparently about why TV was such a great industry to invest in, and in particular, how he felt that investors did not ascribe value to the programming. What actually makes people switch on a TV set to watch a particular channel is the programming. That perception that Coronation Street, that Granada made and owned, was hugely valuable because it attracted 20 million viewers a week, and yet investors did not appear to be aware of that intangible asset. That was an idea that I took directly from Buffett. For me, when I look back at the ideas that created the outperformance, that was a massive, massive one.

I think your question is a very good one. And I think that for me, I would say that the truth is that capital markets are tending towards efficiency. By that I mean the academic sense of everything that is known that can be known is reflected in prices. I do not think they are completely efficient but they are definitely tending towards efficiency.

Therefore, ineluctably, however disagreeable this may be as a proposition, the only way that you can earn exceptional returns is by doing something that is not in the price, something that is not in the market. That is what Sir John was saying – "I did this, it was against the run of conventional common sense at the time, it was very painful for a while, people thought we were mad, but actually in the end we were right." It is an inescapable fact about capital markets that if you want to do well, you are going to have to take risk, and have to take some pain as well.

LG: Let's talk about Buffett. "Stocks are simple: all you do is buy shares in a great business, for less than the business is intrinsically worth, with managers of the highest integrity and ability. Then you own those shares forever."

NT: There are two aspects of this that are really important for us – and this does not necessarily mean that they ought to be important for everybody else, but for us they are.

The first is this straightforward proposition: invest in great businesses. At one level you might think, well, what a truism that is. Of course no one is going to invest in anything except a great business. But actually, that is not true is it?

23

People do invest in all sorts of businesses of all different qualities and calibres, and often with great success.

People will say, "Well, we knew that this was a pile of rubbish but the price was so cheap that it couldn't go down anymore and we made a great return". That is a valid approach to the investment challenge. I know people who have been very successful who have done nothing but look for what Tom Dobell's M&G Recovery fund does. It is a perfectly valid, time-honoured approach.

But it is not what Buffett has done and it is not what we choose to do. We think that investing in very good businesses makes a lot of sense. So our research efforts are just concentrated on finding what we think are exceptional things. That helps us understand where we want to focus what we do.

The other aspect of the Buffett quote, and the one that I know when I discuss it with people and when people hear us talk about it, they think is just flippant, they think it is just a Buffett joke, this idea that you hold things forever. There is a bit of north-western US humour in that. But I think he was deadly serious actually. Because everybody knows that stock markets are volatile, everybody believes that the ideal way to deal with that volatility must be to persistently be selling at the top and buying at the bottom; it must stand to reason that because it is volatile, the best thing to do is to treat the volatility. That is fine except no one has worked out how to do it.

Actually, what Buffett says, in all seriousness, is that the best investment is one that you never have to sell. Or that you could hold for a lifetime. The absolute ideal would be buy something at the price of one and then in 20 years' time it is worth 50. That is the ideal investment. Who cares if it fluctuates a bit during the course of that?

So again, with all awareness of our fallibility and the fact that we make mistakes – and we will make more mistakes in the future - we are trying to invest in assets, or companies in particular, that we are hoping we can own for a very, very long time, if not forever, where we have got a chance that they might turn from one to 20, or 40, or 50 over time.

LG: And in that longevity of holding a stock, what is the role of the dividend, the reinvestment of the dividend?

NT: Well the academic theory says that dividends should not matter. It says that actually if the company that you are invested in has such fantastic opportunities over time to grow, you should not want it to pay a dividend. You should want it to invest everything back into growing its own business.

We take a more pragmatic view. Although we are very supportive of companies if they say "Look, we have got a fantastic reinvestment, we would rather not grow the dividend this year, or for a couple of years because we think we can do something better with the money". That is fine from our point of view. But identifying a great business is in the end a matter of opinion. There is nothing statistical that proves that something is a great business. It is a qualitative judgement.

For us, a long record of a steadily growing dividend is strong corroboration that something probably is a fine company. We are very interested in a company's really long-term dividend history. Even if we are aware that a purist might argue that it is irrelevant or maybe even the company has made a mistake growing its dividend that much. But in the real world, where you do not know for sure that something is a great business, seeing that is a comforting proposition.

LG: The other part of Buffett's quote is about managers of the highest integrity and ability. How do you judge good management?

NT: I don't know that we ascribe quite the same significance to individual management teams that Buffett suggests there. We know that over our investment time horizons, there are probably likely to be a number of chief executives and a number of chairmen at the companies. And we know that they cannot all be geniuses.

The way we look at this is that we tend to have a clear idea when we invest in a company about what is special about the business. We are constantly looking for comments, and more particularly actions from the management of the companies that they share our view.

LG: So would it be right to say in a sense that you look for management who you think mirror the way you look after your investors' capital?

NT: What I am about to say goes against some consensual thinking in my industry. I think Mike [Lindsell, co-manager of the fund] and I do fall in love with some of the companies we are invested in. We really, really love the idea of owning a measurable proportion of the London Stock Exchange. It really excites us to think that our clients have an ownership claim on a fraction of such an incredible asset. So yes, I think that is true of a lot of brands. I have known Young's the brewer since I was a child virtually. I live in south-west London. Every time I go to Richmond, I look at the White Cross Inn, a freehold property, and I think that is a fantastic site for a pub and my clients own a piece of that in perpetuity. There is a strong sense of us having ownership of some of the underlying assets within these companies. And yes, I think you put it very well, when we talk to management or watch what management are doing we think about whether they share our enthusiasm and the desire to nurture these rare and wonderful assets.

LG: And the last bit, stocks are simple. I don't think he's saying businesses should necessarily be simple to understand. But you have invested in businesses like Sage; that is not a simple business is it?

NT: I understand something about Sage; my business uses it. Put it this way, Sage is a lot easier to understand as a technology proposition than many others, in my opinion. If I were to say something dogmatic, I would say that for anybody whose business or whose personal wealth depends on selecting individual shares, in individual companies, I would say it was unforgivable to invest in anything that you really do not understand. And I think that is what Buffett was saying. You have a responsibility. If you are picking individual stocks there is no excuse for not understanding what the company does. That is something I have tried to follow.

I have said in the past, I personally think that we are in the early stages of another huge bull market in bio-technology but I have also said that if any of our clients see me buying a bio-technology share, they should sack me, because I know not the first thing about the science of bio-technology.

LG: So Peter Lynch, the classic five baggers and ten baggers. He said a couple of five baggers every decade is enough. "In my investing career the best gains usually come in the third or fourth year, not the third or fourth week" was his line.

NT: For someone of his attainment and achievement to say that, I just thought that was an amazing thing for a professional investor to say, and so true.

LG: That quote was from 1994. You were about 10 years into your career. Do you remember hearing it that around that time? Did it really resonate with you and clarify stuff that you knew but had not quite articulated?

NT: I think I have had two bites at Peter Lynch. The first time I read *One Up On Wall Street* – the second book is also very good, *Beat the Street*. The first thing I got from Lynch was this idea of find out what your wife is buying at the supermarket. That is valuable investment information. That is probably more valuable than your in-house economist telling you that M3 money supply is expanding by 6% next month. To actually know when your wife says, "Do you know, I have just been to M&S and this season's fashion is rubbish". That's a more valuable piece of investment information than a piece of macro gibberish.

So that was really important to me to understand that they are companies you are investing in and the companies have customers. What Lynch says in the books is so true, that the amateur private individual can be just as successful observing the world and what is working and what is not working as these guys sitting in their ivory towers playing around with their black box statistical trading machines.

So I think that was the first thing I got from Lynch. Then much, much later we were thinking about what it means to own a successful investment for five years or seven years or 10 years and after a while, if you have picked well, it doubles, and then it doubles again, and if you are really lucky, it doubles again. I dimly recall that that was what Lynch did, that was what made him so successful. I think I have talked about it, he had these 10 baggers. One hundred 10 baggers. Amazing. But I went back and I re-read it and in a sense it goes back to one of the oldest pieces of advice in the investment industry which is run your winners. In a sense, that is all Peter Lynch is saying, run your winners. To me, that is such a powerful observation.

LG: So you don't work to a price target for selling a holding?

 NT: I think what Lynch is saying, and I feel the force of this myself and it is still very hard to deal with, is that there are enormous psychological pressures as a participant in an equity market, amateur or professional. There is enormous pressure to do something. There is particularly enormous pressure to take money off the table when something has done well. I do not know why that should be such a deeply instinctive visceral thing but you feel "it has gone up, I really ought to take some profit".

I think what Lynch is saying and what he demonstrated with his career was that actually you can take the fact that a share has gone up as a signal that there is true value creation going on in this business that could go on for a lot longer than you anticipate. The rising price actually might be a sign that you ought to be buying more, not taking the profit. Obviously everything has to be leavened with some sort of perspective and common sense. But knowing that worldly-wise professional investors are supposed to be taking profits here and re-investing there, and not obviously generating consistent wonderful results from doing so, I just thought that was a really powerful counter-statement to that tendency.

Acknowledge that the price target that you have set is virtually arbitrary. Particularly if you are invested in a rare company that is doing something that other companies cannot do and making money out of it, do not part with it lightly. Because for every one of those, there are 200 mediocre businesses that are floundering around, trying to work out what the hell to do next.

LG: The best gains usually come in in years three and four. How long do you hang on to an investment that is not working?

30

NT: We have never been able to work that out. So, at times to our intense annoyance and frustration and sometimes to our clients' intense annoyance and frustration, we have just tried to be as purist about this as we can be. I think of a business like Reed Elsevier, which in 2013 actually worked for us. But we have been persistently nibbling away at an investment in Reed Elsevier, probably for 10 years. And for nine out of the 10 years, it has been disappointing. But we know a lot of other investors would have just thrown in the towel – maybe correctly, frankly, who knows – years ago and said "this will never work, let's find another idea". But – and I am not saying that it makes us better, maybe it makes us more dull – but for us, as long as the intellectual case that we were investing in, so far as we can tell, remains intact, we will just keep biting the bullet and adding to the holding.

LG: There is no arbitrary time target from your perspective on when something stays in or goes out?

NT: No. Again, and this is more of an overly contextual comment, neither Mike nor I are under any illusion about what we do. We do not think that we have solved the answer to the investment challenge. We do not think this is the alchemist's stone; we know it is not. We know we are fallible, we know that every investment approach is fallible. All we think we can do is try and stick to a set of principles, in as pure a way as we can, accepting that there are times when we will do things that are stupid, because we have stuck to those principles. But so much of what looks obvious is obvious because it is in hindsight. At the time it is not obvious.

LG: Let's move on to Vivian Bazalgette, former CIO of M&G, who said, "Whenever you find a company that makes products that taste good you should buy their shares."

NT: This links back to the Lynch idea of paying attention to what your wife says about what is selling well in the supermarkets. Sometimes simple things, almost so simple that people would overlook them, can be the most powerful. And the piece of advice that Viv gave me is at one level absurdly simple and yet when you think it through and actually when you invest on the basis of it, the returns have been fantastic. So Viv's advice was when you find a company whose products taste good, then you should buy the shares. How ludicrous is that in a sense? But I really have genuinely tried to think of and find a counterfactual to that. I have actually looked through lists of companies around the world and in the UK that make products that are acknowledged to taste good and try and find one that has not worked as an investment. And I cannot find one.

LG: Is it stretching the advice, the taste element, to take into some of the other ideas that you have in the portfolio?

NT: Yes, maybe. One reason why we have held on to our investment in Hargreaves Lansdown is we just know so many individuals who anecdotally say the service is amazing. So in a sense, that is tasting Hargreaves Lansdown's product. But I would not, for the full force and for the money-making potential of that piece of advice, stray from just your taste buds. That is powerful enough as a piece of advice.

It is harder to do it in the UK. Stuff that people enjoy, that is probably a good place to start, thinking about investment. No one really enjoys buying insurance. Or banking. In October (2013) 154 million visits were made to Mail Online, up 44% over the last 12 months. Love it or loathe it, it is undeniable that that is something that people are wildly enthusiastic about.

But this fundamental idea (of buying things that taste good); Buffett's purchase of Heinz Ketchup (in February 2013). Okay, he did it in a joint venture. But that deal probably goes back 60 years, maybe longer, to him dipping McDonald's fries into it and thinking that tastes good. That is just a really powerful model.

LG: Now Richard Thornton, one of the founders of GT; "Great money-making ideas are rare; make sure that when you find one, you make it count."

NT: Well, when Richard died in February 2013 I wanted to find a way to acknowledge him and the gratitude I felt to him and the influence he had on me. That obviously is a somewhat flippant quote. But what I would say is that what he was looking to convey to us then and what he lived by as a professional investor himself was this: that truly, truly exceptional investment ideas are quite rare and you should never forgive yourself if you do not back one of those relatively rare ideas properly. You can wait a long time for the next one to come round – yes. I think particularly for a professional, you have really got to back it if you believe in it.

LG: When do you know that it is a truly exceptional idea?

NT: You can't. Maybe it comes from experience, I don't know. But associated with this (and I think this element of it perhaps is more helpful for all types of investors including amateur investors), I think the flipside of what Richard was saying, and again, he was explicit about this, is that one sure route to mediocrity is having too many holdings. If you let ideas proliferate, after not very many, you are much better off just to buy an index tracker. You are just wasting your time if you have got 75 half-a-percent holdings, or whatever. You are not doing anything, it is not worth it. You are just guaranteeing mediocrity.

LG: That concept now of diversification has almost strangled investment portfolios?

NT: Again, I go back to what I was saying about Templeton at the outset, that there are cheap, very cheap and effective options available to investors who simply want to get performance to the average share in the UK stock market. And those are quite compelling I think. For those of us who claim to be and set ourselves up to be active managers and who have the effrontery to charge the fees that we do, although I must say I think our fees are certainly low by the standards of the industry, but nonetheless, we are charging more than a tracker, then I feel it is utterly beholden upon us to offer some value, potential value, for that extra fee that the client is paying. For us that comes from backing our judgement with a relatively small number of names.

LG: The Leonard Licht (of Mercury Asset Management, now BlackRock) quote: "Never invest in any company that makes anything out of metal". Does that just appeal to you?

NT: Yes, it is a brilliant quote. As I say, you will know who I mean, it was actually told to me by (Artemis's) William Littlewood, who worked for a period with Licht and I did not hear that from Licht, so it is second hand, so I want to be careful with it. What I took from that, and maybe it is somewhat in a historical context, but investing in what are inherently cyclical, low return on capital businesses like metal bashers is a mug's game. I think that is what Licht was saying. And maybe after extraordinary efforts, maybe you can earn a return out of it but the risk you are taking by persistently investing in low quality companies, it is hard to justify when there are good companies out there that you are not taking the same risk.

Whether he would say that or whether I would say that in precisely those words today I am not sure, because that was probably said during a time when a significant proportion of the UK stock market was still populated by metal bashers or let's say textile companies. I cannot remember how many times people heralded Courtaulds or Coats Viyella; this time round the company is better run. And in the end, bless them – and God, it must have been terrible working there – the companies were just what they were. They were never going to be able to escape from the curse or the sentence that had been imposed on them of being metal bashers.

What is left though, what has survived, I know full well that a Weir Group or a Rotork, these have been fantastic investments over the last decade because they were clearly doing something of value and had survived and that was an important signal. So I am not sure that exactly that terminology would be the right thing to say today, but the message in my opinion of "do not waste your time trying to value inherently low value-added companies" is a good one.

Chapter 3

The Committed Investor

Andrew Green interviewed by Lawrence Gosling

Andrew Green is longevity personified having been at GAM – where he now runs the Global Diversified and UK Diversified funds – since 1983. He is a committed Christian who says his faith helps him ignore the "noise" of the world of investment and avoid being swamped by the highs and lows of market swings.

Before joining GAM, Green worked under the legendary investor Nils Taube (1928- 2008) at stockbroker Kitcat Aitken where he says he learnt the lesson that the worst mistake of investing is having an over-active portfolio.

Lawrence Gosling: What brought you into managing money for private clients?

Andrew Green: I have always been interested in statistics and as a teenager I used to follow share prices by plotting them on graph paper, which is very sad. I therefore had an interest in why things happen. I applied for a job in stockbroking and it just went from there. I was very fortunate to come under Nils Taube when I was 21 and so I had his influence in the first 15 years of my career. He was one of the great post-war investors, having come here as a refugee, escaping from Estonia, first from Nazis and then the communists. He, along with George Soros, were big names in the '50s and '60s. He took me under his wing basically and gradually I absorbed the thinking of avoiding consensus.

LG: Were you conscious of the lessons that you were learning from Nils?

AG: He wasn't that type of personality. I would have to question him: why are you doing this? And I'd get a half sentence as he bolted for the door. But as we got to know each other and the friendship developed, we would go out for a drink and he would talk more openly about things. Around about the same time, I became a Christian and that was very important in my philosophy of not thinking the noisiest voices were true, because you won't get any great knowledge from information being thrown at you.

It's interesting; it's not long since the 50th anniversary of T. S. Eliot's death, and one of his famous quotes was about the superfluity of information not leading to knowledge and that knowledge itself doesn't lead to wisdom. (Ed note: The full quote reads: "Where is the wisdom we have lost in knowledge? Where is the knowledge we have lost in information?")

So along with all of that thinking is not to trust a lot of what you're being told but think it through in terms of what you understand to be true as opposed to what everyone is shouting from the rooftops is important. The combination of those two influences spawned the philosophy that goes against the grain, not to be perverse but to look behind what we're being told, to try and understand if there isn't something else going on that we might be missing.

LG: Would it be wrong to describe you as a contrarian?

AG: Unfortunately it's a word that I think has become corrupted because people talk about being contrarian as simply buying something that has gone down, or whatever was unpopular last year must be popular this year. Reversion to the mean does play a part in it, but the canvas we paint on is probably as long as half a century. Now obviously that's slightly dramatic but the charts I use would span that period. You can see at a glance how the behaviour patterns of investors over those decades have culminated in peaks and troughs for various reasons.

If there's been a trend in something maybe for several decades, you might start asking a few questions as to whether it's gone too far, what might change it, how this might occur and so on. That's how we approach investing money, not in a short-term view, but actually very long term. We all have spasms of short-termism because we're human and investors, that require you to respond to certain things, but ignoring the at-the-margin stuff, it is essentially a very long-term process.

LG: Presumably one of the things that you learnt very early in your career from Nils would be this concept of accumulating returns steadily over a longer period of time?

AG: Yes, because obviously every time you churn, you're losing the dividend stream. And of course, as we know over the last century, it's basically the accrual of dividends that has driven the performance in a general market sense. Plus whatever the fund manager adds or subtracts from that. So the worst sin of fund management is over-activity, because you have the powers to say yea or nay on every investment every day and the immediacy of all these things buzzing around in front of your eyes on screens does drive that. I think I saw that most markedly in the run-up to 2000 when the dotcom boom was almost at its peak. The movement was just extraordinary. It can grip you, I think, and much of it was nonsense.

LG: During the course of your career there have been investment fads and there always will be in markets. How do you combat being accused of being basically an old fuddy-duddy?

AG: I remain one. I felt that in the early stages of 1999. I thought, "I've clearly lost it, I'm not seeing something and I can't understand this; no-one cares about multiples anymore." I remember having lunch with Nils at the time and he said: "I feel like Ulysses; I'm lashed to the mast by my fellow managers because I've let them run, have their heads, because they seem to know and they are young and bright and all that sort of thing." And I thought, "Oh golly, even he has succumbed'. And it was right for a while – and then totally wrong and he very much regretted it. But we can all feel old, fuddy-duddy and vulnerable and therefore you cede power at the wrong moment because it does seem very convincing. It wouldn't have its power if it didn't.

LG: Did you get the same sense in 2008 that things were looking just wrong?

AG: Oh absolutely, and that is why I feel so aggrieved that we didn't do better, because we avoided any banks. That was where the issue was, we could see it; it was going to implode, most of the banks. And therefore I stupidly thought one was safe by just avoiding that sector. But actually there were other things that came back to bite us and you basically had to go for the most dumbed-down portfolio you could imagine, of utilities and consumer staples and so forth. That was a failure on my part not to realise that. But we all need to be humbled by events. In a way, I look back and I am relieved because it would have raised expectations even more.

LG: How much does your faith play a part in the way you run money?

AG: Yes, obviously I'm prayerful about how I do my work. But I think there's another element to it in terms of the despair or the greed, if you like, that mark the highs and lows of markets. The presumption of blue sky and the despair of dark market crashes, both of them might overwhelm the normal human thought processes but you need to keep those balanced.

LG: In your experience, have some of these trends in the markets got shorter since the turn of the century?

AG: Well it's a funny thing actually, but I've been seeing the opposite where low interest rates have actually extended this cycle. In prior cycles, higher interest rates curbed inflationary bubbles and the build-up of excess debt. Once this happened, recovery names tended to perform well. This time round, the system has not been completely reset, which has meant that solidly run companies with earnings streams that are easily extrapolated into the future have become more highly rated. And the ones who might have been the recovery stocks in the old century are dragged further and further down because they don't have a way out of their debt. That I think upsets a lot of what are called recovery funds because recovery hasn't come in that sense, in that way.

Everything has gone on much longer and I think the mistake that I've made in the last year or so is assuming, when you're taking profits, that it's not going to go on, and it has. It goes on. We were right to come out of small caps and mid-caps but a lot of things have just stayed on a par without being challenged, because there weren't obvious alternatives.

LG: Tobacco stocks would be an example?

AG: Absolutely, 30 years of outperformance of that poisonous weed. At the same time, you can see the ground shifting under their feet as sales dramatically fall and yet they manage to push up profits each year because they always tack on an extra margin with the tax increases. But in the end, it will topple over.

LG: So over the years when you've realised, perhaps, a mistake that you've made with an idea or a cycle in the markets, how do you try not to make that mistake again in the future?

AG: Well, one very clearly should learn from one's mistakes, but of course there is something in one's own make-up and my weakness is trying to judge the bottom of something. Whereas I remember Nils always saying I should always leave the first 20% to someone else. I'm different in that regard.

LG: Would you say you sell too early sometimes?

AG: Yes, definitely. Because if you're in early, you tend to think, "Gosh, this has been amazing." Yet another thing I have learnt over the years is that a different sort of investor will start to look at the stock as I'm leaving, because it's now back into investible territory. And that was amazing to me because I hadn't thought of it that way.

LG: Go back a little bit, over the years, what are the key metrics that you've used that have stood you in good stead in terms of analysing individual companies and where do you get your original investment ideas as well?

AG: Well that does come from the technical side and it's fed out to the team to make the case in fundamental terms. That's really how we work, how we mesh the two together. People have often kept them separate; I think they're very closely linked. These very long-term charts generate the thought process about what we should look at, and then the team will go away and dig into the fundamentals.

LG: Chartism in general is perhaps not as popular as it was. An observation is that over the years, the managing of money has gone from being an art to being very scientific and perhaps you're a mixture of the two. Would that be fair?

AG: Yes, I think there is that element. I can see patterns in investment which other people may think is snake oil. And that's fine. Nils would always tease me and hold the chart upside down, and say, "I can't understand this". Charts can be useful in terms of market timing in the short term, but the short term cannot determine what stocks you would buy. You must think on a much, much bigger frame. My team are able to give credibility to my madness; that's the theory.

LG: How much longer do you see yourself going on for?

AG: I was thinking about this in one of my Bible readings this morning. Retirement is a modern construct but I think as long as the Lord gives me health, he has given me the gift to do this; clearly I won't be able to do anything else as far as I'm aware. So I might as well keep on doing this as long as I'm able.

LG: Do you enjoy it? Because it sometimes seems a lonely place and quite a responsibility to manage anybody's money?

AG: It is, it is. I always say love–hate because you think, "Why do I put myself through this?" But there is the intellectual challenge of working out what's going on and I think that holds a fascination for me. We're all humbled by events because we're not in control of the future, but I think I have a tool here which helps me to make some sort of sense of where we are, and I obviously get it wrong but not as many times as one gets it right. So on balance, you're probably putting a plus sign in over the years. That's the aim. I'm always amazed when people say I absolutely love the business, because I think it's terribly difficult.

LG: You've mentioned Nils quite a lot, but who are the other fund managers that you respect, admire, and have learnt something from?

AG: I think [Fidelity's] Antony Bolton, I know everyone will quote him, but he wasn't just an accumulator of assets, which I think some of the famous people today are. I think he was amazingly right on a number of cycles, over a long period of time.

LG: It strikes me he almost invented the recovery or special situations portfolio.

AG: Yes. I think it's astonishing the number of companies he

45

would see every week, which I don't, that's not part of my process, because we wanted to operate in a different way. But I admire him. And I think coming back and having one more trip round the track in the Chinese investment process was a clear challenge and it was a reminder to all of us that the "roar of the greasepaint, the smell of the crowd", is very hard to give up and not keep doing it, because it does absorb you intellectually.

LG: Do you follow or ignore a benchmark when you're investing?

AG: Well I really wouldn't totally ignore the benchmark because that smacks of arrogance to me. So I'm always aware of it without being a slave to it. Obviously at points of extreme valuation like technology we can ignore it. But most of the time, you don't get that clarity. And therefore, you have to be humble in the face of that and say, "Well, I'll have to pay respect to various sectors and have something there, till it becomes clear." Then I would vacate whatever it might be.

LG: How did you come to run your own fund?

AG: When Gilbert de Botton [founder of GAM] formed the company, I expected him to say I want you to run a UK fund but he said, "No, I want you to run a global fund". I said I knew nothing about global investing and he said, "I think you just apply the skills you've got across a broader space." I would list him as an influence. I don't think personally he was a great investor, but he was clearly a visionary in terms of building a company in a niche area that wasn't fashionable at the time and creating something very, very successful.

LG: What are your thoughts on China?

AG: Everyone knows where the risks are and what they're trying to do to stem them but clearly it's not an easy area to invest in, both from a technical, legal, regulatory perspective, and from the point of view of not having invested in China before. Also, I think it's important to recognise the old chestnut that GDP growth and trends don't determine stock market returns, certainly not in anything other than the very long run.

China has a clear opportunity to reform, and reform plus supportive valuations are a positive cocktail. China is taking the pain in terms of social reform. It's trying to do many things that are, at least on the face of it, friendly to equity holders over the long term. Following the pattern of more mature markets that have made similar transitions suggests the next step for China is the liberalisation of financial markets and when that happens it tends to be bumpy but it also creates opportunities. It is important to realise though that the extent of reform has to be balanced against the fear of civil unrest which haunts the political system.

We have a far deeper understanding of Japan, where our investing history spans 12 years. There have been lots of small positives in Japan in terms of shareholder-friendly moves, which considered alongside the cash-rich nature of corporates suggests there is scope for money to be returned to the shareholder. This is a fundamental long-term driver, we believe.

Chapter 4

The Technology Investor

Katie Potts interviewed by Jane Wallace

Small-cap tech specialist Katie Potts admits to finding life a bit lonely in her specialist investment field. Having founded the Herald Investment Trust back in 1994, she hoped to be investing in the best of British technology, companies that would grow to become global players. She bought into the shares of Apple at $1.46 after a sandwich lunch with the CFO in California in November 2003. Then it was a loss-making, unloved company which had nevertheless just invented iTunes. In sterling terms, the investment has increased by some 100 times.

A concern over unemployment in the UK was a driving force behind the establishment of the Herald investment trust in 1994. Katie Potts, then a technology analyst at SG Warburg, had lived through rounds of redundancies during her first job after university. She had studied Engineering Science on a GKN Group scholarship at Oxford and went on to "make wheels" at GKN Sankey. Having seen the impact of job losses on that company, she did not want the technology sector to experience a similar fate.

She says: "I thought that the only future for the sector was to encourage small companies in the hope that some of them would end up big."

At the same time, she realised there was value in the smaller company sector, especially when the representatives of the large firms were the sluggish BT and GEC.

Creating a fund solved the problem that dealing with smaller companies did not generate the levels of commission achievable from large caps. With the overhead structure at Warburgs, small firms in isolation were not economically viable.

Potts says: "My investing clients found small companies difficult because there wasn't enough liquidity and too much stock-specific risk. A collective, however, would offer a spread of exposure in a bigger vehicle which gave full liquidity."

The project seemed to strike a chord. Potts found herself oversubscribed and having to scale back commitments from £95 million to £65 million. Happily, there were plenty of opportunities to be found in the IT services sector of the time. Firms such as Logica, Systems Designers (now SD-Scicon) and Misys were among Herald's early holdings.

Unfortunately for Potts, not all of these firms lived up to the ambitions she had for them.

She says: "Sadly only ARM has broken through into the FTSE 100. The good news is that we've made good returns; the bad news is that we've done that through takeovers rather than by making big companies."

After two years of investing solely in the UK, Potts realised that she would have to make the fund global, in line with the technology sector itself. She raised another £30 million for the fund and started investing in America. The weightings in UK and Europe, however, stayed at 50% or below so the fund would be eligible to be held inside a PEP – the tax-efficient wrapper for personal savings, now revamped as the ISA.

When these rules were relaxed in 2001, Herald could finally be fully international. But Potts had already dropped the UK exposure below 40% in the first quarter of 2000.

"There are so many more companies and opportunities elsewhere in the world that I thought the weighting would never go back up again," she comments.

Fifteen years on, however, that prediction has not come to pass. The portfolio is over 60% invested in the UK as valuations here, according to Potts, have been too attractive to resist.

Jane Wallace: Herald's been going for over 20 years. Has anything changed since you launched the trust?

Katie Potts: I started with the investment case that there's more growth potential in small companies but it is difficult for generalist fund managers to reach because of the lack of liquidity and the high stock-specific risk. That hasn't really changed.

However, the major difference is that there seems to be a greater shortage of capital at the small end. This is a bit of a hobby horse of mine but I think the regulator has described illiquidity as risk and, for various reasons, people have been driven out of small caps. It's as much the asset allocations of the City that have caused all the takeovers and the lack of small companies becoming big as anything else.

In the last few years, we've had masses of takeovers. Herald has lost £308 million in value in takeovers in the last eight years. It was really scary in 2008 because we had a quarter of the portfolio taken over at very poor prices. And more would have gone if we hadn't vigorously defended them. I can think of a couple of examples where there was a takeover announced and we bought in the market above the takeover price to try to stop people accepting.

So why have there been quite so many takeovers? Obviously companies compete when new markets open up. A parallel with the web development companies could be the motor industry. In the 1920s, there were about 250 car manufacturers in the UK and as a sector matures, you end up with fewer players.

At one level, it's what you'd expect. But what has upset me, given my original motivation, is that none of the aggregators have been British. Invariably the takeovers have been to foreign companies or private equity. I used to think that venture capital invested at the early stage and then exited via the public market. In recent years, it seems we've become public ventures and sold out to private equity. There's no doubt people have been able to be more creative with capital structures because of low interest rates.

JW: Does that make finding smaller companies more difficult?

KP: No, but it means we're forced down to smaller companies because the bigger ones have been taken over. And just to explain why it's a hobby horse of mine, have a look at the UBS Pension Fund Indicators' annual survey of asset allocations in UK pension funds. It shows that the UK used to be 60% of people's portfolios and now it's gone down to 30%.

I did tell the Prime Minister, David Cameron, about this at a lunch I had with him – I hasten to add there were about 150 other people there. But I did explain that UK investors are selling UK equities hand over fist: Is it a vote of no confidence or is there some other problem?

I'm not sure that it's because we're anti-UK. The fashion has been to globalise and whereas people used to have UK equities as a benchmark, they now have a global equity index.

People have sleep-walked into it without realising what effect that has on the UK economy. If the biggest owners of the market halve their weighting, there's a huge overhang of selling. Figures from the Office of National Statistics show you that the rest of the world is the biggest owner of UK equities – just over half are in overseas hands. And it's doubled in value from 1998, going from £460 million to £935 million.

If you change tax, you change behaviour. There was actually a tax incentive for pension funds to own UK rather than foreign equities before Gordon Brown abolished the recovery of ACT on dividends and made a level playing field. So suddenly for pension funds, they get tax relief on fixed interest but they don't get tax relief on dividends. Then there's an incentive for them to own, say, corporate bonds rather than equities. Combined with low interest rates, that's created the private equity and the leveraged buyout industries.

On the other hand, it's been an opportunity because, when there's an overhang, stocks are too cheap. The UK has been full of creativity and entrepreneurialism but on the whole it's been commercialised by US companies. So, if there's such a crummy little sector in the UK, why do we still have over 60% of the portfolio here? And the answer is that stocks are too cheap in the UK.

I also think we're one of the few people prepared to invest so the exposure also provides capital for jobs.

JW: So how would you describe your investment style?

KP: It's very bottom up. Top down, I say Asia and America, and bottom up I say UK. If a Taiwanese company, a UK company and a US company come through the door, we buy the company that we like the most, not the geography.

JW: Is there anything you look at in particular?

KP: I like business models with defensible margins. On the whole, companies which are good to work for are good to invest in because they have pricing power. And pricing power often comes with intellectual property, brands and market share positions which give fat margins and also added-value jobs.

JW: How did you play the tech bubble?

KP: I took a lot of money out of the UK. There was actually more of a bubble in the UK, and even more in the Neumarkt in Germany, than there was in America. The American sector was so much bigger, so there wasn't the same liquidity squeeze upwards. But there was a bubble everywhere.

Then the UK market collapsed and the tech sector was down about 90% from peak to trough. There were actually some really interesting opportunities. Lots of companies had been seeded in the tech bubble and they hadn't got enough money to get to profitability. So I bought and then they rallied very strongly.

We had a fantastic year in 2003: the NAV was up 76%. Then we had a relatively bad performing time between 2004 and 2006 when our NAV went sideways. I was very frustrated at the time because the companies were performing really well but the share prices were not rising as much as profits.

In hindsight, I comprehend that it was a dirty great credit boom and it was more attractive to fund managers to buy house builders on P/E ratios of seven in house building, property or mining.

The tech sector is not as interest-rate exposed because there's not much debt in it – it's not like houses or cars where people buy on tick. Relatively speaking, it went sideways. But then we outperformed very significantly in the downturn because the financial crunch hit the credit-driven sectors more.

There was another spectacular buying opportunity in 2008. We didn't exploit it quite as well though because, as far as I am concerned, we wasted £40 million buying back our own shares – we were on a wide discount. And that's frustrating because the whole point of an investment trust should be that it's long-term capital.

JW: What about risk in the portfolio? These companies can blow up from time to time.

KP: We try not to own more than 10% of a company. Occasionally we will if a company really needs cash, but I would have to go to the Board for that. I also don't like buying 10% of a company that's loss-making. You want to have room to add if they need more money.

We also have a spread of companies – about 270 – which we manage in four portfolios. The UK portfolio has about 150 companies. We tend to go to smaller companies in the UK more than elsewhere because of the need for capital and because AIM (the Alternative Investment Market) exists. There isn't an AIM in the States, for example, so there aren't so many very small companies.

When I joined the City, everybody looked at companies from first principles to a degree. Now I think fund management is done more by top-down asset allocation. You've got ETFs, you've got index trackers, so an enormous proportion of funds aren't actually managed on the micro-understanding of a company and whether it has potential to grow. People are lazy. When you're managing billions, why waste the effort on small companies where you can't put that much money in? It's more important to get the asset allocation decisions right. So people don't bother.

On the one hand, it's frustrating that there isn't enough capital, and that companies get taken over too cheaply. On the other, you get a takeover premium and can invest in something else too cheaply. But it means we're not giving a good enough return to the seed investors. That's not good in the long run because nobody will invest in early seed stuff if they don't get a return.

There's got to be a change so the stock market is viable as a sensible owner of companies. In the past, I would have always advised going to the public markets for long-term capital – not to private equity because they have their own agenda and they'll want to sell out. Unfortunately the public markets haven't been good shareholders for the last few years. It's not just the techs. It's Cadbury and lots of other companies which have been sold just for people to get their weightings down.

JW: So when do you sell your stock? What makes you decide a share price has gone far enough – either way?

KP: The cash flow statement from last year shows that we sold £109 million worth of stock but we had £60 million in takeovers. So about half the sales were involuntary. Elsewhere, most of the money was taken out by some of the more mature companies which grew to valuations we found quite expensive. That's one of the tensions we face between solid companies which have become expensive and very cheap, risky companies. We have to decide how much we can increase the 'risks' by going into more early stage firms. But that's why we have a lot of holdings.

It's hard to think of a FTSE 100 company which can double on a two- to five-year view. At the smaller end, as far as I'm concerned, the risk–reward is a lot more attractive because you can only lose 100% but you can make 1,000%. That's the whole point of being able to give people a relatively low risk way of getting exposure to riskier stocks.

JW: Do you exit a stock when it hits a certain valuation level?

KP: A crude P/E measure isn't sufficient because you pay a much higher P/E when a company is just getting into profits. Growing the margins from 1% to 10% makes a much bigger difference than a company whose margins have reached a more mature phase and can only grow in line with sales.

Induced by the regulator, the perception is that big caps aren't risky and small caps are because of liquidity. But actually if Facebook's value is $150 billion, there are different risks. Can it become worth $300 billion, can it be worth $1.5 trillion? Equally there's an awful lot of value that can be lost.

I have an open-ended fund as well, which is large cap, and I own Google but not Facebook. Google seems to have a much more solid business model. Being the dominant search engine, it's so powerful. Whereas advertising to kids … the scary thing is that fashions can come and go. I think Facebook is too risky to own. The downside could be 90%, even 100%. But the chance of it going up 1,000% is nil.

JW: Are there any other investors who you admire?

KP: I feel incredibly lonely in the UK. There were more companies which we would have funded but we couldn't find enough co-investors. I genuinely wish there was more competition.

As far as the tech sector is concerned, Polar are pretty serious. But there's probably zero correlation between our portfolio and theirs because they're more into the Apples and Googles of this world.

When I started Herald, we would sit behind people like Prudential on the share register. Now there really aren't very many of us: Hargreave Hale, Anthony Cross, Liontrust and maybe Gervase Williams. I'd say Hargreave Hale more than anybody else tends to have stakes. Often we're the biggest investor in small companies.

I remember, when I was at Barings, hearing a county council trustee say that small companies would create jobs and that part of the pension should be allocated to small companies. You don't hear that comment or that attitude today, it's quite the opposite: the actuaries have pushed people to have a global mandate.

So the investors left in small companies now are almost entirely retail, either directly or through people like us. And in retail funds, cash flows come and go. That's why the stock market has become a rather unhealthy shareholder. Because if the UK private punter is getting nervous about the market and has decided China is more fashionable, they'll sell. That's outside the control of the fund managers. Even if they know the companies are solid, they have to sell if they've got redemptions.

Pension funds are the ideal long-term owners to provide a solid, stable shareholder base but they've been driven out of the market. I think the actuaries and the regulator have made forced investment decisions without really understanding the economic ramifications. I'd almost say they've vandalised the UK economy.

JW: What's the major difference between the tech sector now and 20 years ago?

KP: There has been rotation. The sector I joined was defence and telecoms. Then it went into IT services: Logica and all those companies peaked in the millennium bubble and then the sector moved to India.

I've spent my career watching manufacturing move to Asia and IT services to India. There's actually been some signs of repatriation because companies realise that the cost–benefits aren't quite as good. Skilled people are becoming higher paid, there's very high staff churn and then there's the inefficiency of communicating with people who are on a different time zone.

For manufacturing, you've now got so much progress in terms of automated machine tools set against the six weeks it takes to ship from Asia. And the cost of capital is the same anywhere.

China has become the manufacturing industry for the computer sector. You can argue that tech is now a much bigger proportion of world GDP because of the spend on PCs and phones. It's possible that, as it matures, it'll be like the automotive industry where demand goes on but it's more of a commodity and slightly more cyclical.

The internet has grown like a weed because it's free. Companies like Yahoo knew the cost of storage would be a killer and they had to have some free form of it. That's why they've created Hadoop, an open standard like Linux. It will potentially be disruptive for the likes of Oracle as people migrate from legacy databases for which they're paying big maintenance fees.

JW: What's the best thing about being a fund manager?

KP: The interesting people you meet. We're incredibly privileged to be able to quiz chief executives around the world about their businesses. For me, investment management is the hobby and the job is coping with the regulator and the accounts.

I have an added kick to my job which is being able to deploy capital usefully. It's really fulfilling if you've given money to a company which was incredibly grateful to get it because they were struggling to raise funds. It's a virtuous circle: the company's grateful for your money and your investors are grateful because you've made a return. We are genuinely making the cake bigger rather than being clever at taking a share from somebody else.

INVESTOR TIPS

For investing in small cap tech stocks

1. Select businesses with defensible margins. These firms tend to be characterised by a strong brand, intellectual property or dominant market share.

2. Liquidity does not equal risk-free. Large companies can also collapse, experience financial difficulties or struggle to grow.

3. Look for companies with pricing power. They have the ability to create large margins and high-paid jobs.

4. The rise in internet usage has been matched with an increase in electronic crime. Security will continue to be a growing market.

Chapter 5

The Small Companies' Man

Harry Nimmo interviewed by Jane Wallace

Harry Nimmo found his calling in the smaller companies universe via Saudi Arabia and analyst work at Standard Life, looking initially at US equities. Now co-manager of the Standard Life Global Smaller Companies fund, with AIM as one of his hunting grounds, he suggests that the 20-year-old market is perhaps the best example of a buyer-beware market. "At least half the AIM index is made up of conceptual or blue-sky investments," he says.

Sitting in a caravan in the desert, Harry Nimmo realised he needed a new career. He had spent three years surveying for the national oil company, Saudi Aramco, and had made a decent amount of money.

The hours were long, 60 to 70 a week, but there was no tax and nothing to spend his relatively generous salary on. But something was missing.

"The pace of development in Saudi Arabia looked a bit unsustainable and the future Mrs Nimmo was not to be found there. I had to think of something else," he says.

Nimmo had worked hard to build up his cash reserves

and they turned out to be his exit visa.

"I was so greedy for money that I used to trade in my leave to bank the spare air tickets and make even more money," he explains, "so I was fortunate enough to be in a position to finance my way through another university qualification."

Nimmo had already been investing his Saudi savings in equities and, back in early 1980s Edinburgh, an MBA seemed to be the natural choice.

His studies decided him that asset management would be a sensible career, especially as it was a growing business with a lot of activity locally in Edinburgh.

It was, however, harder to get a job than he had assumed. Having sent his CV to about 50 companies, he got only five interviews and plenty of polite rejections. Just as he was considering returning to the Middle East, Standard Life offered him a position on the US desk as a trainee analyst.

Aged 28, Nimmo was starting again from scratch and on a considerable cut in pay. "It seemed perfectly worthwhile to do that," says Nimmo, "and so it turned out to be."

The head of US and Nimmo's boss at the time was John Thomson, a talented manager who would go on to become chief investment officer. Thomson took a shine to his new junior and, five years later, when Thomson was made head of UK, Nimmo transferred across with him as a large cap analyst. Three years later, Thomson offered him the job of head of smaller companies.

This was, on the surface, a poisoned chalice.

Nimmo explains: "It wasn't really going anywhere. And it was all entirely internal money; there were pretty much no third party assets. The 1990s were a very difficult period for smaller companies."

The problem was that many smaller companies were in fact distressed larger companies, 'mostly manufacturers suffering from the decline of the UK's industrial base and cheaper competition abroad.

Coats Viyella, for example, was one of the biggest small caps in Nimmo's benchmark in 1993. It had been the largest company in the world before World War I. "It was a company with a great future behind it," comments Nimmo.

By the end of the 1990s, many of these firms had gone bust or disappeared, causing small caps to underperform large caps during the decade.

Nimmo recognised this was a historical anomaly as traditionally small caps have provided better returns than their larger counterparts.

He says: "I saw the time was right for smaller companies. I don't think I foretold the turning point but certainly, on old-fashioned valuation terms, smaller companies were quite cheap and unloved relative to other assets."

Other factors convinced Nimmo that small caps were due a recovery. There was a flurry of large cap mergers, particularly between the banks, which Nimmo doubted would actually add value.

"I do see it as a kind of a collusion," he explains. "If you're a chief executive and you can make your company a great deal bigger, you're going to get paid a great deal more.

65

And investment banks get paid fees for completing deals – the bigger the deal, the bigger the fee. They're not really interested in the long-term success of the merger, they're just interested in doing the deal."

Since then, it would appear this theory has been borne out as smaller companies, where there is less merger activity, have outperformed large caps.

Nimmo explains: "A corporate culture is very important. If you disrupt that by throwing two similar size companies together and sacking lots of people, everybody is watching their back, not the business."

Eventually Nimmo was given the go-ahead and Standard Life launched a small cap unit trust in 1997, just in time to catch the first upswing in small caps in late 1998. Their outperformance has continued relatively consistently ever since.

Influence of technology
As the old industrial businesses which populated the small cap indices fell away, new firms replaced them. The technology bubble did puff up and then burst but many innovative operations emerged from the aftermath.

Nimmo explains: "Smaller companies in the main could quickly take advantage of the new style of doing business, whereas larger companies with their legacy infrastructure and assets were left high and dry."

Notable examples of this can be found in the airline industry. Online booking allowed easyJet and Ryanair to break through, leaving behind national carriers like Iberia which were slow to embrace e-commerce.

Investment process

There are about 700 small caps in Nimmo's investment universe so a screening process is essential to cut down the analysis legwork.

Once the universe has been whittled down to a more manageable short list of around 150, company visits to cross-check the accuracy of the screen can take place.

Nimmo's screen is referred to as "the Matrix" and has been developed for smaller companies over the last 20 or so years from the core Standard Life investment philosophy of "What's changing?"

He says: "We use it in a very systematic way. Nothing works all the time, but we have found that this has been effective through four different market and business cycles."

The process is not so efficient in a recovery phase, especially after a long bear market. Often the inflexion point of an upturn occurs when sentiment is at its worst, as was the case in early 2009. A sudden realisation in the market that the pessimism had overdone led to a big rebound in the very riskiest stocks – where of course Nimmo was not invested.

He explains: "These are strong periods for smaller companies generally because they are seen as a slightly riskier, more cyclical asset class. So our fund goes up. It's just that when our benchmark goes up by 50%, we only go up by 40%.

Although being 10% behind benchmark "looks like a complete disaster", Nimmo has discovered that the bulk of his investors are unconcerned.

"They think 40% is pretty damn good," he said. "And they actually like the resilience we provide in bear markets." For example, while UK smaller companies declined some 60% in the period from June 2007 to December 2008, the Standard Life fund went down less than 40%.

Nimmo abides by six rules for investing in smaller companies. The first and most important is to look for sustainable dividend growth. This is achieved through identifying stocks with growth potential, quality financials and earnings momentum.

Nimmo explains: "We're looking for businesses which can grow in a sustainable way or have visibility of earnings. In terms of quality, we want to see a strong balance sheet and cash flow to match, along with management that doesn't take high risks with shareholders' equity."

Another indicator of quality Nimmo uses is the Altman Z-Score, a form of credit analysis. This composite of asset, balance sheet and cash flow measures has been found to signal relatively accurately whether or not a company will survive. Nimmo will avoid any stock which fails this test.

Great attention is also paid to earnings momentum. This data is collected by sell-side analysts whose forecasts change over time in response to newsflow and changes in the fortunes of the companies.

"We find a tendency towards persistency in the trend of the analysts' forecast, both on the way up and on the way down," says Nimmo. "You want to get on board with a positive trend."

Nimmo will also look for barriers to entry, pricing power and market share which, to his mind, are evidence of a strong business going forward and one which can sustain its growth.

He explains: "The share price of a stock is based on its prospects for profits and dividends. That changes all the time, for better or worse. We're trying to identify companies where the outlook for earnings and dividend growth is improving. That's rule number one."

These kinds of ideas actually contradict some academic theories, Nimmo says, particularly the efficient markets hypothesis. This theory suggests that it is impossible to "beat the market" because stock markets are so efficient that all the relevant information is incorporated into share prices which therefore always trade at fair value.

"Our thinking is that they are plain wrong," he says. "Active management is possible and you can add value through diligent research. The market is not actually that brilliant at discounting all the information and providing the perfect equilibrium for share prices."

Concentrating the effort

The end result of feeding all the data into the Matrix is a "score" for each stock. Nimmo will look to buy stocks with high scores – and sell those in the lower rankings. By doing so, the fund is skewed towards the higher scoring stocks. As each of the UK, European and global funds will typically be invested in just 50 to 65 stocks, this makes for a concentrated portfolio.

Nimmo explains: "We don't care about the 550 stocks that

don't have high scores. We are doing rule number two –
concentrating our efforts – on the stocks that have the
characteristics from our Matrix that suggest outperformance."

On the other end of the spectrum, if a stock gains a low
score from the Matrix, it is a signal to sell. The hard reality of
numbers on the page helps to override any emotional
attachment of the fund manager to a stock or its management.

"At the end of the day, we're there to make money for our
investors. So we shouldn't be too loyal to the corporates."

The third of Nimmo's rules for investing in smaller
companies is to select quality firms. While this seems like
common sense, it is in fact a risk mitigation tool which,
according to Nimmo, is often overlooked by other fund
managers.

"If smaller companies are a high-risk asset class, why not
invest in a lower risk way by picking firms with strong balance
sheets and sustainable businesses?" he says.

In stark contrast to the received wisdom which equates
risk and reward, in his own experience, Nimmo has found
there to be no such correlation between the two.

"If anything, the lower the risk, the better the reward in
smaller companies," he contests.

In fact, Nimmo has found several areas of hegemonic
thinking in the investment world which he is keen to
challenge.

"Investment practice quite often follows outdated and
discredited academic basic research," he argues. "Efficient
markets theory has now been discredited. But, because the

powers-that-be trained under its sway – including myself, I might add – they stick with it."

He adds that some derivative pricing models were based on efficient markets templates, including the Black–Scholes model. One of its originators, Myron Scholes, won a Nobel prize for the theory. However, when the principles were put into practice via the hedge fund Long-Term Capital Management, the result was the spectacular failure of the fund in 1998.

"What more discrediting do you want?" comments Nimmo.

One of the most obvious hunting grounds for nascent firms is AIM. Two decades down the line, the index has never quite shaken off its reputation for roguish listings.

Selecting quality stocks is paramount here because, as Nimmo puts it mildly, it has always been "a bit *caveat emptor*".

"At least half the AIM index is made up of conceptual or blue-sky investments," he argues. "They have no revenues, no profits and no dividends. They are often just an idea, and turning an idea into a sustainable business is incredibly difficult."

Radical new technology ideas or firms which have "found" new reserves of oils and minerals are often very attractive but often do not make money. Nimmo's advice for avoiding the duds is to check whether the firm pays a dividend and if it has any revenue. If it does not, his advice is not to invest.

Nimmo himself has fared well in the AIM market with plays such as ASOS and Abcam. Around 20–25% of Nimmo's UK fund is typically invested in AIM shares.

"There are some wonderful AIM investments. But there are also promoters who can talk a good game. Just a great story attracts the money and it certainly did in the tech bubble."

Longevity

Continuity is an important factor in smaller companies investing, both for the investor and the investee.

"The best way of making money in smaller companies is holding great companies for extended periods," says Nimmo.

For the fund manager, that means both running the winners (Nimmo's rule four) and searching for management which will stick with the firm in the long term (Nimmo's rule five).

While some investors see management change as a catalyst to a poorly performing business, Nimmo does not subscribe to the view that a new boss can always turn a firm around.

"I'd much rather be involved in companies with stable management and particularly with certain individuals who are real business builders," he says.

Much store is set upon company valuation by fund managers but, intriguingly, not by Nimmo. In several decades of back-testing and refining his investment process, he has discovered valuation is not as predictive of future performance as some managers believe. This insight is his sixth and last rule.

In today's world, newsflow is relatively immediate and reliable. In the main, Nimmo finds a stock is lowly valued for a valid reason. It could be financially troubled, cutting its dividend or having a profits warning.

Instead, factors like director buying and rising price momentum are more reliable signals of potential good returns.

Nonetheless, Nimmo does include valuation in his calculations: "It keeps you honest and dilutes the impact of some of the blue-sky stocks which turn out to be less than they seem."

Brand value, although without an official place in Nimmo's Six Rules, is still a priority for consideration. Consumers can often spot declining service standards or a fall in quality and will consequently switch to another brand.

Nimmo identifies this as more of a problem for large or mega companies which, at a certain size, have to be creative in the way they can return value to shareholders.

In the beer market, for instance, Nimmo interprets Brazilian brewer AB InBev's large appetite for mergers as a means of rebooting stalling growth.

Other methods companies might use to boost the bottom line include squeezing suppliers or resorting to cheaper ingredients. Such value-engineering, however, provides opportunities for smaller companies, Nimmo points out. If the large fizzy drinks manufacturers choose to swop sugar for the cheaper chemical sweeteners, a small firm like Fentimans or Fevertree can step into the taste gap and grow rapidly.

During 30 years of fund management, Nimmo has picked many winners but, inevitably, also some losers. From one company in particular, he learned a hard lesson in transparency.

Software firm AIT was a top ten holding in Nimmo's UK fund in 2001 with a weighting of around 2%. It transpired that the executive chairman, Carl Rigby, had been falsifying trading statements to the stock market and earned himself a prison sentence of over three years for doing so.

Nimmo reflects: "It taught me that just because a seemingly honest person is telling you that everything is okay, it doesn't always mean that it is okay. Particularly if some of the circumstantial evidence going around in the market is not okay."

Six rules for making money in smaller companies
1. Look for sustainable dividend growth.
2. Concentrate your efforts.
3. Go for quality.
4. Run your winners.
5. Management longevity.
6. Valuation is secondary.

INVESTOR TIPS

Private investors are the most likely to be seduced by blue-sky investments often proposed by oil prospectors and tech start-ups, just the sort of money which should be focused elsewhere, according to Nimmo.

"If you really want to make a lot of money, you're best to avoid these companies," he says.

Instead, identify those small firms which actually make money. This research can easily be done via the internet, usually from the company's own website, which will provide much of the relevant financial paperwork.

"You'll get most of what we get," says Nimmo. "You won't get a face-to-face meeting with management, but you'll get everything else."

STANDARD LIFE UK
SMALLER COMPANIES SAMPLE STOCK
ASOS

Harry Nimmo first invested in the online clothing retailer ASOS back in 2006 when general market sentiment had turned against internet stocks.

Founded in 2001, the company had five years of history and was profitable. But more importantly, it was a "mould-breaker".

"Everybody went from loving the internet to hating it as an investment. But there were a few stocks that came through with great disruptive business models and ASOS was one of them," says Nimmo.

The entry point for Nimmo was an unfortunate event for the firm. An oil storage depot at Buncefield blew up, taking the roof off the ASOS warehouse with it. Fortunately ASOS were insured and were back in business after only a short period.

Nimmo says: "After that we saw that the business was still a good business: well-financed and growing rapidly. So we took an 8% stake at that time when the market capitalisation was £60 million and the share price was 80p."

The holding was bought slowly over time and was eventually sold down between 2011 and 2014. During 2014, the average exit price was £47.

The investment, however, was a rollercoaster ride with the share price halving on several occasions.

"In our terms, it was above average risk," admits Nimmo, "but it had a proper business when we got involved."

When the stock started to show a negative score on Nimmo's screening Matrix, based on falling earnings forecasts and slower growth generally, the decision was made to sell.

Chapter 6

The Englishman in Europe

Richard Pease interviewed by Lawrence Gosling

Richard Pease's start in the industry was a modest one, first running funds for the Church of England. He soon progressed joining Jupiter in 1999 and subsequently at New Star in 2001 to run European funds, and all despite not speaking one word of French or any other language. Latterly, he spent six years running the European Special Situations fund at Henderson Global Investors before switching to a brand new fund management venture called Crux Asset Management which he established in the summer of 2015. He comes from an 'investment' family. His sister is Nichola Pease, also interviewed for this book, and his brother-in-law is the well-known contrarian investor and hedge fund manager Crispin Odey.

Lawrence Gosling: What are your earliest recollections of money and investing?

Richard Pease: In rather ridiculous ways, I tried to supplement my pocket money. Most of the schemes went horribly wrong. One of them was to try and breed tropical fish and sell the little ones. But that certainly wasn't a success. My sister Nichola and I had quite a good little side business in silver coins. Pre-1967 (silver coins) were half silver and pre-1920 it was all silver. When the silver price went through the roof, the content of the silver was something like three times the value of the coinage. So that was quite a little earner and was the best of the businesses I had, but I never did share dealing.

LG: So were you destined for a career in investment after university?

RP: My academic career was never particularly distinguished. I started off reading geography at Durham and got kicked off the course, which was rather embarrassing. Then I ended up doing general arts. I think I got a very decent degree in the end, but it was a relatively good recovery from a very bad start.

I was pushed into working for what was then called Knight Frank & Rutley and with all the right intentions. But I must have been one of the very few people who were sacked from Knight Frank, for being completely inept. Thank God I was; I spent my hours in some rather dingy windowless room, sticking maps together. From a career point of view, it was a bit of a cul-de-sac.

Nepotism came to the rescue in the end; my uncle was incredibly pro-family and at the time was chairman of an organisation called the Central Board of Finance for the Church of England, which ran quite a lot of money. There was an incredibly nice guy who ran it called Victor Churchill, and I got a job running a very straightforward deposit fund. You couldn't go hugely wrong. I upgraded to a small equity fund and went from there. It was actually an incredibly good grounding, funnily enough. It was extraordinarily badly paid. It meant that you had to do Personal Account dealing just to be able to pay the bills actually. I had about three years there and it was great fun.

LG: So was there somebody formally teaching you the ropes?

RP: I never really had what would be regarded as any kind of formal training in anything. I think the only thing I would say is that we had a very nice chap who I suppose was the main guy there, Andrew Gibbs, who was a Methodist, and he did sort of missionary things. He was a very dry accountant really but actually with quite a good sense of humour. I got on quite well with him.

I was quite lucky in a way because I came across quite good analysts. We were sufficiently mainstream to attract decent broking houses and I was lucky enough to fall into the right sort of crowd. You pick things up over time like that, making some mistakes along the way but I never went horribly wrong, and the little fund I ran did reasonably well. I began to realise actually relatively early on how important it was to have guys who cared about shareholders.

This was a time when you had all these big companies with no one really focused on the shareholder at all. You began to realise that the guys running these businesses didn't even remotely rate shareholders. The cost of equity was just the dividend yield they were giving you, very miserly at the best of times. It was a bit of a wake-up call. Once you had a couple of those sort of things happening to you, you thought, "Crikey, we've got to back the smaller businesses, the mid-caps where guys actually own some shares." Luckily I picked that up relatively quickly.

I think the other thing one picked up was that it was very important to make sure you were in the same class of share. Because you had some family companies where they could really abuse you, because they had the voting stock and you had preference (shares) and they could do anything they liked, essentially. So you had to try and find the ones which worked because you were all the same class of share.

LG: Did you find you learnt stuff because you had an empathy for it?

RP: I think I've been very, very fortunate in the sense of the company I've kept. We were all very naive in many ways but then we didn't have to be brilliant because the market was unsophisticated in so many ways. There was not a lot of research in some of the mid-caps and the accounts were very often not even in English. If you had a good Dutch analyst or good German analyst or French analyst, you could probably get what was very good information in a very imperfect market. I remember I had a lot of small/mid-cap Dutch stocks at one time because my sister focused on Holland, we were buying these things on single figure P/E multiples. They were growing really quite fast actually. There was a period when it was very easy to make quite good money.

I was quite lazy in many ways, but at the same time it was one of those things where the more you did, the more fun it became. It was rather like desperately revising, swotting up for an exam, when you suddenly realise actually it's quite an interesting subject.

I left Central Board of Finance to join a very nice friend of mine who had been working with me there, called Simon Baker. He offered me this job at a thing called Windsor Investment Management, and they gave me a European mandate. I was never going to get a European mandate at the Central Board of Finance because I couldn't speak any French, essentially.

My little European fund did very well but I had Nichola to give me all the right ideas and it was actually the top-performing fund, which was quite amusing really because I was not particularly good at Europe when I started but I just did what I was told.

So I'd met John Duffield (founder of Jupiter), who was at the time trying to launch an investment trust himself, and we got on quite well actually. It was slightly ridiculous. I said to him, "Have you got a European side?" and he said he didn't. So I remember saying, "Would you like me to start one?" and he said, "Yes". I said, "When would you like me to start?" and he said, "Next week". That was the interview. So then I was very much in at the deep end. I had to work incredibly hard because I was doing pitches to Soros and Tiger Fund

Management and everyone in New York. I really didn't sleep for about two weeks. It was the first time I was desperate.

LG: Going in to see Tiger – you must have felt like you were bluffing your way through it?

RP: Oh yes, completely. I think the saving grace was Julian Robertson (founder of Tiger Fund Management) is incredibly nice, Very, very classy. I would say that to anybody, he was really good and really nice. The mercy was we had a lot of meetings and so each meeting only lasted about 45 minutes so one could never be absolutely hammered in 45 minutes, as it were. Your time was an irrelevance for most American investors; they'd give you the time of day and I was reasonably well prepped, I did nothing but work for two weeks. But it wouldn't have borne up to some fundamental interrogation.

LG: What was essentially 'the story' you were offering them?

RP: It was just when the Berlin wall was coming down; we were going to focus on some of the opportunities that had arisen. Valuations in relative terms to other parts of the world, and particularly the US, were on big discounts. It was Europe awakening essentially. We were really pushing the five- to ten-year story because we thought the starting point was very attractive, particularly in Germany. You were moving from bonds to equities, there was so much to do and it shouldn't have been hugely difficult to benefit from all the things that were going to happen. That was the story.

The truth was, of course, it wasn't a one-way ticket and the reunification came with huge costs and the problem is you just didn't have a level playing field. What is quite clear with hindsight was the dishonesty about some of the structures, with the voting shares and prefs and things like that. The other thing which one didn't really appreciate was the dead hand of the State which very often had the controlling stake in these big companies. In particular if you go somewhere like Italy, they were political appointments. The board was very much in the gift of the politician, they were always doing something for somebody. That meant that you were very disadvantaged. So that was the challenge. But you could find these little mid-cap Dutch stocks or Scandinavian stocks where the valuations were very modest and they could do all sorts of sensible things.

I hadn't really appreciated that fully at the time because I hadn't done it for very long, but you were waking up slowly to that. We raised a very small amount of money, I think it was £6m, which wasn't very much.

LG: Did you ever stop and think, "Blimey, I'm the guy who got fired by Knight Rutley and is now looking at millions in European equities"?

RP: I think in my case I grew up very slowly and I think that the reality was that it was quite helpful to have a job which didn't matter. Because if I'd started off doing what I do now,

I'd have probably fluffed that too. You had to grow up, for want of a better description. But I just was a slow maturer really. And I've been lucky because there are various crossroads and you can very easily go the wrong way and I was lucky enough to go the way that worked for me. I was lucky enough to have a lot of friends in the right places at that particular time, which made it much easier.

LG: It must have been more than just luck?

RP: I suppose if I was going to try and give myself credit for something, it would be that in the end, you get quite good at working out who to back, whether it's the good analyst or whether it's the good CEO. If I was going to add value somewhere, I think it's probably more in that sense. Because I think a lot of people can do the spreadsheets and they can analyse the quarterly numbers until there's nothing left to analyse, but if you are backing a guy who is fundamentally dishonest or incompetent or hugely exaggerates, no matter how much analysis you do, it's not going to work out in the longer term.

You've also got to understand what kind of fundamental businesses you should be in. I think a lot of people get sucked in because they think something's a bit cheap or this time it will be different, all those sorts of stories. Whereas I think where I'd like to come from is what sort of business would I like if I wanted an easy life? They've got to have characteristics we look for, in the sense that you don't want to have to invest huge amounts of capital to get growth which is going to come from essentially much less predictable areas of the world, emerging markets, and that kind of stuff.

LG: Given you don't speak another language, how do you assess the people?

RP: I like to meet them myself. I think luckily, if you have to choose one language now, it's very much English. It's remarkable really because that was certainly not the case 25 years ago, particularly in places like France. That's changed. What gives me comfort now when I see somebody is you want to understand what somebody has done and looking at the track record before you start giving their promises a huge amount of weight.

Certainly when you follow the business or management for some time, you get a very good feel for someone as to whether or not they are, putting it politely, very enthusiastic and tend to be too optimistic in terms of their forecasts. Then other guys who always talk it down but always out-deliver. You can have the optimist but you have got to build that into the numbers a bit.

I think there's no real alternative as far as I'm concerned to see real money from somebody in that business, and I think that you really want to be careful about the guys who just do three or four years and then move on, cash in their options and get a bigger salary. Those guys I'm always much more careful about.

LG: When you meet a chief executive how important is the response when you ask them what their motivation is? What's the balance between them saying, "I absolutely want to maximise shareholder returns," or when they go "Actually, do you know what, I personally could earn €50m over the next five years running this company, I'm going to make sure I get there"? Where's the trade-off for you?

RP: It's never quite as crude as that. Particularly if you talk to the guy who started the business, I will see that he's got 15% or whatever it is of the business, and my question would be, depending on how old he is, essentially whether at some stage they might want to do something·else with their lives. What's the end game for them?

A happy ending for me is either they just stay put or they have good guys running it they trust and they leave their money in. You expect people to take something off the table at some time but I think that's not necessarily a bad thing. But you don't want to be in a situation where basically you're the only guy left on the boat and you think, "Christ, where am I going?" and they've all got out. I'd have been much more concerned about that. But it's very important. If you are a mid-cap where the entrepreneur may have over half the company, it's very much about what that guy wants. It's very important to realise what he wants works for you too.

LG: What do you think in general terms about the investment industry nowadays where it seems like everybody has the CFA examinations?

RP: I'm not remotely saying it's not important but I don't think it's just about the accounts.

I'd like to think I can understand enough to do the job quite comfortably. I very much focus on free cash flow, understanding how you get there. Understanding how they depreciate things and what the maintenance capex is. It's the real world; so how do you pay the bills? Is that dividend safe and do they need to keep on asking me for money because they can't grow the business without investing a lot of money? All those sorts of things. Or are they in a situation where actually the reverse is true? They have got so much money and they haven't got, in realistic terms, the projects to invest the money in because the money is being generated faster than the ideas. But the point is that that's the angle I'm coming from, rather than getting the exact numbers perfectly right, because I don't think it's about that.

Certainly if you're an entrepreneur, it's never really about worrying about what's going to happen this quarter. You are really making five- to ten-year decisions, trying to position yourself, dominating a niche, increasing your recurring revenue, and making jolly sure you've got a powerful bit of niche pricing and that kind of stuff. Your returns on capital and things are going to improve rather than be squeezed. It's much more about that and understanding that in my view.

LG: Do you think the opportunity set is still largely in the small and mid-cap part of the market?

RP: I'm very happy to look at all different market caps but I think what one ought to try and do where possible is to control your destiny as far as you can. I would be very careful about anything which is very vulnerable on regulatory changes. Those sort of things I would worry about. We're not anti the bigger companies at all but we're anti the companies which get squashed by regulation and by politics or just legacy costs.

LG: Do you think Europe's changing?

RP: I always get back to the difference between where you're born and what you do with your life. Corporately speaking. So it's not really about Europe, it's about good businesses which dominate global niches. It's a very, very common mistake that people make I think, but from our point of view, it's the opportunity rather than the problem.

LG: If investors are going, "I've only got so much money to allocate, Richard, why should I being allocating a significant proportion to a strategy like yours?", what's your reply?

RP: I suppose what I would say, actually I always say: "Give me less, but be patient".

LG: Is that just to manage their expectations?

RP: Well I think there's a bit of that because I get asked by friends, "Is this a good time?" And I loathe those questions because the truth is you might think it is a good time, but my approach has never been about timing, it's about buying something which is a long-term winner and having sufficient confidence to stay with something.

I think it's really a question of finding some companies which in very simple terms meet our criteria. Making sure that they continue to meet our criteria; there's no change in a negative sense. And then just being patient. Because if you look at it very simplistically, if returns on invested capital in these businesses are good, if they can reinvest their relative prodigious free cash flow into these sorts of assets, you get the power of compounding. It doesn't always go right; there's going to be bumps on the road clearly.

There's always something which one can worry about. But in a funny way, that's a good thing because otherwise we'd have euphoria, which is a bad thing if you're buying stocks when the markets are euphoric.

LG: You ask people running companies what their motivation is but what is your motivation now?

RP: I guess that it's an interesting job. There's always something to think about and to worry about.

LG: But you can argue it's a really pressurised job, you're looking after money on behalf of thousands of people, many of whom you will have probably never met. You're looking after people's retirements?

RP: I think it's a very good point to make that but all I can tell you is that as an investor in a company, I like to know that if someone gets it wrong they personally lose a lot of their money. And as an investor in my fund, people have the reassurance that that very much applies to me. I've got to answer to my wife as well, by the way. But the point is I think it's very important to taste your own cooking and I certainly do.

From a pressure point of view, this is coming back to the point that I always say to people, give me less than you think you should but be patient, and they panic essentially. What I don't want to do is for someone to mortgage their house to the last degree and stick it all in my fund just before the market comes back sharply. But you can't avoid risk in this life. You've got to understand the risks you're taking. You're taking a risk buying equities, clearly. But I still believe and I really will always believe that if you are in companies which make sense in terms of your business model, run by people who have proved themselves, who have their own real money in the business, and are very competent in terms of making bolt-on acquisitions and that sort of thing, I still believe that the direction of travel is very positive over the longer term.

I guess, yes, I feel responsible but because I'm not hopefully overpromising and I'm not telling people I can clean up over the next two or three months, I like to think we're all adults and I'm honest, I believe in what I'm doing, I've got all my family money really in the fund, and I'm prepared to take volatility because I think the direction of travel is going to be fine. I'm not going to sell out at the bottom. On that basis, I can always look an investor in the eye and say well, look, even if I have got it wrong, you'll know that I'm a lot more affected than you are. But it really is for me very meaningful indeed and it's real money for me.

LG: What's the little nugget or bit of wisdom that you would offer up to somebody who is an investor or potential investor?

RP: I think that it's really somehow trying to not worry about what is essentially a long-term investment over the very short term. I would always urge somebody to invest rather than speculate, because that's what we try and do. If you genuinely get your head around that, and you are investing, not taking some punt, I think then your mind-set is much healthier and you can understand and not worry actually about the fact that the market is down 5% or something, because you have complete belief in the fact that actually these businesses do prevail over time.

Chapter 7

Looking for Growth in Japan

Sarah Whitley interviewed by Jane Wallace

Japanese equities specialist Sarah Whitley joined Baillie Gifford in 1980, became head of its Japan equity team in 2001 and has been running the Baillie Gifford Japanese fund since 2007. She believes investors focus too much on the index and demographics in the country rather than companies and how they are changing.

Jane Wallace: Is investing in Japan very different to investing in the UK?

Sarah Whitley: Japanese culture is fascinating. It is very different from the UK but it's not as different as people think. Our perspective in the UK is very coloured by the fact that people only like weird Japan stories. Yes, weird stuff goes on in Japan, as it does in every other country. However, it does seem to be a particular obsession of the UK media that stories can only be about Japan if they are bad news or something weird.

There are some differences in how society is organised or how meetings function, but I don't think there's anything really radical. When you look down the key companies that have been winners, there's nothing that makes you think – oh, that could only happen in Japan.

It is a bigger economy than the UK. There is a wider spread of companies and the Japanese market has never been as concentrated. I think the top 100 companies in the UK comprise about 85% of the overall market but in Japan they would only be just over 50%.

JW: Did you always invest in Japan or did you start elsewhere?

SW: When I joined, Baillie Gifford was a firm of 35 people. It was like what I call a geek firm – a company where as long as there's enough revenue to pay people, there's no idea of maximising the business. There were some fantastically intelligent and rather eccentric people. I spent my first year sharing an office with Robin Angus, who is one of the directors of Personal Assets investment trust, which was an extremely interesting experience.

I also worked for Max Ward and Douglas McDougall, mainly doing the UK market. The next year, I did the US and then I rotated on to Japan, or the Far East as it was called. There was no great plan.

Japan was quite a dynamic area at the time. We launched the Japanese fund in 1984 and we already had the Japan Trust so there was quite a lot going on.

JW: What do you look for in a company?

SW: We are looking for firms which will grow their business significantly in the next three to five years. It can sometimes be a company which is restructuring, or it might be growth in earnings, if not the overall size of the business.

So we are growth investors. People sometimes find that a bit odd because they always say value has done well in Japan. But I think that's because they define growth as being expensive stocks rather than growth stocks.

JW: Can you describe your investment process?

SW: We look at four main elements and then at valuation. The first is the industry background and then, second, is the company's competitive position. Then thirdly we consider the financial aspects of the business, and fourthly the approach of the management.

Attitudes of management in Japan are far less homogeneous than the attitudes of probably business-school trained executives in the UK or the US. Some of them are very interested in returns to shareholders and some of them are focused on making sure the employees don't have to be sacked. It depends on the strength of the business.

Finally we look at the valuation. We like to do the qualitative work first and then think about the valuation and work out how we might differ from the market at the end of the process.

JW: Does the stock have to meet a certain valuation?

SW: We're not looking for anything in particular, we are just trying to decide if the quality of the business is reflected in its current valuation or not. We're not against paying a high P/E if we think the business is very worthwhile.

For example, in 2014 we bought Cookpad which runs the world's biggest user-generated recipe website. They've got 50 million, mainly Japanese, women signed up to this. They've also bought an Arabic food website, one in Indonesia and one in Spain, which is used in Latin America too.

It wasn't on a cheap multiple but, on the other hand, they're only at the beginning of monetising their business. Now they've started getting supermarkets to pay to send – that means, if somebody looks up a chicken recipe, the local supermarket can send them a voucher for 10% off chicken legs. Quite a powerful thing.

We bought Cookpad because we thought it had huge potential for monetising the existing business and taking it overseas. Then there's the potential uplift in five years or so from the "internet of things". Your fridge could talk to your computer and detail what you have left. Then a site like Cookpad can suggest a recipe based on that and whatever else you need from the supermarket to make it. That's when it will become even more powerful.

JW: How do you structure your portfolio?

SW: Normally we have about 60 stocks in both the Japan Trust and the Japanese fund. They are benchmarked against the TOPIX but we're not very index-aware. Fortunately, there's only a few companies which, if you don't own, can make a difference, like Toyota.

We don't use the Nikkei. It baffles me why people still use this pre-computer age, price-weighted index, rather than a market cap-weighted one. I suppose it's the one that people have heard of and it hasn't been displaced yet.

We have tried reporting the portfolio in industrial sectors but we found that, with the more internet-related companies, similar stocks appeared in different industry sectors, which wasn't helpful. We have moved on to look at growth styles – secular growth, real stalwarts, special situations and cyclical growth – rather than particular industries.

JW: Do you hedge the currency?

SW: We did, 20 years ago, but we haven't done it for a long time. You need to have a strong conviction that you have a process which gets it right. Yen/sterling is quite an odd rate because it's not very tradable, so you need to get yen/dollar right and then get dollar/sterling right, and then you think – maybe not.

We do what we're good at: finding fantastic companies to invest in for the long term. It's not right to take additional risk. If they know we're not doing it, investors can take out their own hedging out if they want.

JW: When do you sell a company?

SW: We tend to sell things when we're sure. We look at our original investment thesis to see whether it has been proved wrong or played out. We don't sell a stock because it's gone up and there's a scare story on it. We wait to see whether that's right or not.

It's quite easy as a growth investor to take profits too soon. You can make good money sometimes by being a bit more patient and not thinking "I've made some money on this, I need to reduce my holding in it".

JW: What happened in the so-called "lost decade" and has it been resolved yet?

SW: The market peaked in December 1989. I think it was 3,900 on the TOPIX and it went down a long way. The market was very concentrated: it was completely dominated by ideas from a few domestic brokers. It was not a pleasant market to be investing in because the fundamentals for the companies didn't matter. I remember coming back from a trip and thinking that I may as well chuck my notes in the bin because it didn't make a difference. And that's a bit depressing.

After the bubble burst, there were huge deflationary forces working on the Japanese economy. Growth was extremely slow. But, if you look at real GDP per capita, it actually kept up with US figures until, what was called in Japan, the "Lehman shock". It was a long, slow adjustment which resulted in lower asset and consumer prices. But it didn't mean that nothing happened.

In fact, there was a rise in civil society. Tokyo has been vastly improved with several new metro lines being built and big, glamorous areas developed like Roppongi Hills. Marunouchi, which is a central office area, used to be full of dreary 1960s blocks. Now it's got a lot of very swish half-shopping and half-office buildings.

Also during that period, company fundamentals became much more important. It was a better time to be trying to outperform the index. People need to disconnect from the index and consider what the fund has done. Has the fund made money for people over long periods of time? The answer is yes. So it doesn't matter what the index has done because the index is a construct, it's not a portfolio.

JW: Is "Abenomics" the answer?

SW: Abenomics is more about trying to break the deflationary mindset which is why it involves massive quantitative easing. Japan didn't do QE when the US and the UK did, after the Lehman shock. That caused a lot of pain because the currency appreciated and manufacturing in Japan became very uncompetitive. The government realised they needed to join in so they printed a lot of money. Then they started talking about fiscal flexibility but actually they did a major tax increase and now they're considering fiscal stimulus to support the economy if necessary.

The most significant move has been deregulation, particularly the introduction last year of the stewardship code and this year of the corporate governance changes. Japanese companies are quite good at managing the P&L, whatever the general perception is in the West. But they haven't been so good at managing the balance sheet so there's been more focus on return on equity (ROE). We're going through the AGM season and ISS have advised voting against managements where ROE has not got over 5%, or has been below 5% for several years. So companies are beginning to focus more on ROE as a metric and we've had the new index, the JPX400, which requires a certain level of ROE for inclusion. There's a slight feeling of shame for companies if you're not good enough to be in that index.

It's formed an incentive for companies to start thinking in different ways. Some firms might be considering using their cash pile to buy in shares while others could actually stop doing bad business. We get about 200 companies a year visiting us – we don't select those, they're just the ones that want to come. You see some pretty bad companies, but they're the ones that are changing. The corporate governance rules aren't going to make a bad company into an excellent company, but maybe it's going to turn a bad one to mediocre. And those which are mediocre to good.

JW: Are there any other reasons for change?

SW: Yes, there is a large labour shortage and there has been a huge rise in inbound tourists.

Unemployment in Japan is 3.4%. That's fantastically low. More women are employed in the workforce so some of the slack has been taken up. And many people who retired at 60 have been asked to come back. But there's only so much you can do. However, there's quite a lot of informal immigration from China and other parts of Asia.

Inbound tourism is also having an effect. In May, it was up 49.6% year on year because a lot of Asian tourists are travelling to Japan. When people go on their first trip, they mainly go to Tokyo or they might go to Kyoto. If they're Chinese, they buy goods like rice cookers, Japanese nappies and baby milk. They know food standards in Japan are high and they trust the Japanese brands.

Then they come back on a second trip and perhaps they go further out into the rural areas. The countryside in Japan is quite elderly because many of the young people have moved to the cities. So these areas are suddenly seeing some action where nothing has happened for 25 years.

One of the companies I went to see was talking about crowd-sourcing work, such as to web designers, for example, and those other jobs which can be done online. It's possible that people living in a beautiful part of rural Japan can get paid a professional salary because the broadband is good; they don't have to move to Tokyo. That begins to change ideas too.

JW: What is the investment case for Japan now?

SW: People are obsessed with demographics in Japan in a way that's bizarre. Investing in Japanese companies does not mean just investing in domestic Japan. An increasing proportion of sales of Japanese-listed companies come from overseas so you are really investing in the world via Japan.

Japan will have a productivity miracle in the next 5 to 10 years. Even though they will have more immigration, the working age population will decline and so they will need to become more efficient.

Everyone always sees the demographic decline resulting in demand falling but actually there will be greater efficiency. Part of the reason for higher productivity levels in France and in the UK might be because employers have to pay more – therefore you don't pay anybody to not do very much. There's a feeling that some people in Japan are not, well, you can see it, in the most productive jobs. I think that's going to change on a 5 to 10 year view.

JW: Japan was once a giant in the electronics sector. Can it happen again?

SW: It won't be in TVs and videos, but it may be in robots. SoftBank has just announced a tie-up with Alibaba and Hon Hai in humanoid robots. SoftBank has been developing a robot called Pepper which can interact with people. They've been used in the SoftBank phone shops to greet customers and offer advice. Ever since we saw it, we wanted one for our department. And we've just heard they are finally going on sale in Japan next year.

It's interesting that SoftBank are going to open source the code so that people can develop their own applications for Pepper.

That sort of area is possibly a source of growth for Japan but people aren't thinking about that now. The narrative is still all about Sony, the big disaster, and all of Japan is like Sony. As I've explained though, Sony has some strengths. TVs and so on have gone to Korea and the Japanese are no longer involved in that, but there are many Japanese companies making components for electronic items. Japan is still very competitive in cars and ship-building. It's not quite the simple narrative that people want.

JW: Do you speak Japanese?

SW: No, I'm afraid I'm pretty monoglot. There's quite a lot of people on the desk who are learning Japanese. But actually one of the major initiatives by Mr Mikitani at Rakuten (the e-commerce company) over the last few years has been to make English the company's official language so they can communicate better internally with their overseas companies. There's been more thinking in companies about that, and also about using the overseas employees more equally. So rather than having Japanese bossing other people around, they can use the human resources better across an international firm.

JW: Is there a new generation of entrepreneurs coming through with these ideas?

SW: There's a wish to focus on what entrepreneurs can give Japan. The whole idea in 10 years has gone from "entrepreneurs should be locked up" to "entrepreneurs should be sitting on government committees and influencing policy".

It's a huge shift. I'm sure that's enthusing younger people in terms of where they want to work.

INVESTOR TIPS

Understanding the 'contract' between the company and its customers can be important to picking a good performing stock.

That 'contract' is more complex than just servicing or pricing, according to Whitley. Other factors like brand can play a part too.

She says: "You have to identify the real nuts and bolts of the business, rather than just the top-line description, because that can make a real difference as things evolve."

Running shoe brand Asics is one such example. Whitley notes that, instead of sponsoring megastar athletes, the firm has backed amateur marathons to increase its brand awareness. Performance, not style, has been the focus.

Whitley explains: "Our poor desk assistant once told us that she had bought a pair of Asics shoes and found they were much better to run in. She couldn't work out why everyone was falling about laughing. That's why we bought the shares – that sort of difference."

Another illustration would be Fuji Heavy. Whitley invested in 2012 after discovering they had grown sales in America every year since 2007 – in contrast to most US manufacturers.

Fuji has been successful because, uniquely, all its cars destined for the US market are four-wheel drive.

Whitley says: "They've kept promoting this and thinking about the brand and grown their market share. It's not so much about making the cars as trying to think about how people perceive the cars."

Chapter 8

The Investing Pioneer

Sue Round interviewed by Jane Wallace

Sue Round is a rarity in fund management, not because she is a woman, but because she has spent virtually her entire career at one firm. That firm was once called Ecclesiastical Insurance Group before it changed its name to EdenTree Investments in 2015. Round was one of the pioneers of ethical investment with the Amity fund which was launched she says because Ecclesiastical's clients – mainly clergy and their family – didn't have any saving schemes.

Jane Wallace: How did you get into fund management?

Sue Round: I wanted to work in fashion, actually. I wanted to be a buyer. This was in the 1970s and I started off on a management training scheme with House of Fraser – DH Evans in those days. I worked there for a year and a half but I discovered really quickly that it was dead men's shoes. The buyers stayed in their posts for ever and I was in the ladies' day-dress department which was all Crimplene – it really wasn't at all what I had in mind.

My father, who was an accountant, told me I should do business studies because I was very poor at maths. I'd done a business studies course on the training scheme, so I applied for various jobs and I ended up at Philip Hill Investment Trust Management Group (PHITM). They ran a stable of investment trusts – I had no idea what they were – but I went in as a junior analyst. In those days there were no blue books, no screens and no computers until a long time afterwards, although we did have Datastream which was quite a new invention then.

In the days before computers, company reports and accounts were summarised on a card system called Extel. Annual results would be published on a white card and dividend or news announcements were distributed on a yellow card.

As a junior analyst, Round was tasked with managing the Extel cards. It was not a job she enjoyed.

"They came in boxes, every day, and I had to file them. It peaked around March and April, when there was always this really great stack of them. I hated it, absolutely hated it," she said.

Round says: "These days the report and accounts don't really give you what you want in one place. You have to go off and look for other sources. There was some merit in having just the one card with everything you needed on it."

Very soon after Round joined PHITM, Margaret Thatcher won the election for the Conservative party and went on to overhaul the environment for financial markets.

"When the Tories came in, exchange controls were still in place and the dollar premium was something you had to calculate. Later, of course, they freed up the regulation with Big Bang. It was transformative. But I was still so new, I didn't really appreciate the impact it had until quite a long time afterwards."

JW: What triggered the move to EdenTree (formerly Ecclesiastical)?

SR: When you're the manager of an investment trust, and the shares are trading on a discount to net asset value, you become vulnerable. At that time, you could acquire an investment trust and essentially account for it at full asset value. So, if you bought it on a 20% discount, you would actually pay 80% for it and get an immediate uplift of 20%.

It was really a way of creating a back-door rights issue. We lost two or three of the funds that we managed through acquisitions. It was a small business but the remaining funds couldn't support the team that we had.

I was pleased, actually, to move. My boss was a really dour individual, never smiled, never spoke. We worked in almost complete silence apart from the occasional conversation about the market. I'm quite outgoing and I found it really hard to keep quiet. I can beaver away to the nth degree but that kind of environment was not great for me.

So I was made redundant and I had to look for another job. One came up at Ecclesiastical, now EdenTree, in an analyst role. They were based in Fulham Palace which I thought was a really strange place: fabulous building, former home of the Bishop of London, peacocks in the garden and so on. I had my interview with George Prescott, the chief investment officer. We sat on chairs with tea on a tray, but he kind of threw the stuff on the floor and crawled over on his knees to pour the tea. It made me think, "Oh, you're a little bit quirky, I think I could work with you". That was the start of a 25-year working relationship.

JW: You're said to be a pioneer of ethical investing. Was that the thinking behind the launch of the Amity Fund in 1988?

SR: We were selling life (insurance) products, mainly to the clergy and their families, but we didn't have any savings schemes. Most clergymen don't have property and they need to save for retirement and/or a property. An equity-based product was needed. And the idea of having an ethical screen on it sat really well with what they wanted.

So we launched the Amity UK fund. It did reasonably well in that we probably raised a couple of million which, back then, seemed to be quite a lot. Everything was geared to a very low monthly savings plan. I think we've still got £25 as the minimum. It is actually completely uneconomic at £25, but it met their needs.

JW: Is the fund investment style socially beneficial, ethical or sustainable?

SR: It's all of them. In the beginning, ethical was the word that

110

most people recognised. An ethical screen meant you were taking a negative approach, excluding things. The Friends Stewardship fund, which launched about two years before us, was doing that so we took a different approach in that we put in a positive screen. We thought that if you're trying to invest in companies which are helping the environment, or employing good practices, you should be saying that. So you encourage it.

Of course, everybody else is doing it now, it's all part of the ESG (environmental, social and governance) screening that people do. But when we started it was really difficult to get people to talk about their businesses in a way that was not just about numbers. We used to send out questionnaires. Often they would be returned with "I'm not wasting my time on this" scrawled on it. They just didn't get it.

JW: Did that discourage you?

SR: No, I just thought they were stupid. We used to contact the chief executive with the questionnaire, and if the chief executive can't see there are risks, which are not necessarily easily transcribed as financial risks, then they're missing the point.

JW: Was it difficult to persuade investors to get on board?

SR: We got some traction and we had a tied sales force as well. But I wouldn't say it was that easy because we weren't recognised at all outside our core customers. Even now, the mainstream knows we're running ethical funds but we don't necessarily come straight to mind.

JW: Apart from the ethical considerations, what else do you look for in a company?

SR: I'm a great one for yield cover. I obviously look at earnings but I tend to use a pinch of salt because earnings based on analysts' recommendations are driven by different things. So I'll be checking whether the earnings numbers are reasonable, that management has delivered in the past and that they're consistent. The company might not shoot the lights out massively but double digit growth or decent growth is attractive, especially when you know it's unlikely to dramatically change unless they switch their business model or they have new management.

I suppose it's a bit boring but we do take a very fundamental approach. I like companies which can demonstrate a leading edge, either in technology or in market position. High barriers to entry are not that difficult to identify. I'm not necessarily drawn to very high-tech companies because tech is so changeable. You've got to have something that sets you apart in a different way.

It's nice if you can pick the right ones, but it's very difficult. Who could have predicted Google or Apple would turn out as they did? Higher risk, higher reward companies are all very well but I'm more on the picks and shovels end of the spectrum. I would rather be investing in the people who are providing the tools because tools have a longer life span.

And, if there are specialist tools required, then you've got other avenues because tools can be adapted and that gives them a bit of margin.

That's what I like, having some certainty. They may not be the most racy stocks but I still think about the clergymen: they want to sleep well at night. That's why my portfolios typically have that conservation of capital at the heart. I might have a half unit in something more exciting and I tend to have portfolios of 100-plus stocks. I'm not into "your best five ideas" because to me that spells risk. I know other people work to that model, that's fine. But I've been around for 30 years and that's the way I do it.

Why does CSR matter?

Round says: "These issues have financial implications. For a company which is rewarded for share price performance or earnings performance, it's a straight cost to shareholders if you're paying out massive amounts in fines."

She adds that it would also hit the pockets of savers holding those funds which invest in ethically irresponsible firms.

The example of BP and its Deepwater Horizon oil spill in 2010 is a case in point. Round says: "It really brings it home to people that if you ignore your responsibilities, if you go ahead and damage the environment, then you will be made to pay. And pay and pay and pay."

Banking is another industry to suffer the repercussions of unethical behaviour. The sector has been punished by fine after fine, as well as onerous new legislation, in the wake of a host of controversies ranging from LIBOR-rigging to money-laundering.

"The regulation is really starting to hit because it's becoming much more unacceptable, by anybody's standards, to allow that sort of behaviour to continue," Round comments.

With these very pertinent issues tabled, Round sees that the economic concerns of a company are becoming better understood and more integrated with social governance.

In fact, Round's approach has always been to consider the two elements on an equal basis. At EdenTree, an investment idea is investigated at the same time as an environmental, social and governance (ESG) screen is carried out.

"Most people who run ethical funds have a pre-screened list of stocks which meet a certain criteria. So the fund managers actually don't really have any involvement in understanding the issues. For me, that's only half the story. You need to weld the whole thing together. You need to have people who are a bit more tuned into – I hesitate to use the word ethical because I don't actually think it is ethical, it's more about trying to manage your risks."

JW: How do you get exposure to a sector which is performing well but it's screened out? Banking, for example, can't be your number one pick right now.

SR: It depends on the sector. We do think banks provide a social utility so they have a social purpose. Notwithstanding that they've behaved absolutely like shits and deserve to be greatly penalised.

For those sectors where we're excluded, the "picks and shovels" approach is a way of getting exposure. We're not invested in the mining sector, for example, but there are non-mining companies which benefit from its success such as a mapping services company. They could map an area for the mining firms but they also do environmental impact surveys. So they're doing some social good as well as supporting the industry you might be wanting to avoid.

The other way might be through vehicles or equipment – usually they'll have some sort of multi-application. There are many ways to get exposure if you want it.

JW: What's the best thing about being a fund manager?

SR: I like it because it gives me a much greater exposure to the world. You can look at any sector or any industry, and globally. It's not a restricted job and it never ends. There's always something new to read and it's exciting. You meet lots of unusual people and do things – I've been down mines, I've seen all sorts of industries that I would never have seen in a non-fund management role.

JW: You did mention that you weren't very good at maths …

SR: I wasn't good at maths but I got better at using a calculator. It's important to know your limitations and have bright people around you. I have a couple of guys who are whizzos. But they're less inclined to go with their gut instinct. I like to meet people, to sit down with them and look them in the eye and get a feeling about them. And God, I've met some people over the years who – perhaps I shouldn't say. Well, there was one who was a complete crook and made off with all the money.

JW: Was that your worst ever investment?

SR: No. It wasn't the worst. I've still got the worst. It taught me never to rely on the tax environment. It was a company that invested in forests in a tax-efficient way. There were subsidies and you could offset this, that and the other. It did well, it was a new issue and I went for it.

About two or three years on, they changed the rules. Forestry was no longer tax-efficient and, of course, the share price collapsed. The company subsequently morphed into different businesses. It's now called Tandem and it's a bicycle manufacturer. But I keep it deliberately so I can look at my portfolio and see bloody Tandem there to remind me that we all make mistakes.

JW: What was your best ever investment?

SR: We did exceptionally well out of British Biotech. It was a cancer treatment. Normally we don't invest in unquoted firms but with this one I think we went in when it was about second phase. We stayed with it when it came to the market and we did take some money out. But, like all these things, I think it got bought out in the end.

Then there's the ten baggers – the ones where I've made ten times my money or more. Like Provident Financial. This is always one that creates unease with some people. Obviously door-to-door lending is a specialist area. They are lending at high levels. But they provide a service to a part of the market that isn't serviced at all, or very poorly. They do it quite well and in a fair way. It's a different approach to a problem which won't be cured through mainstream banking.

In my view, I'd rather people borrowed and paid more but could see what they're paying. It's key for me that they know if they borrow £10 it's going to cost £12 or £13 to pay it back. As long as they understand that, it's not unreasonable. I don't like people who take advantage and I think the pay-day lenders did. There is a massive difference between those two businesses.

It hasn't been a popular view but don't you think people should be in control of their own affairs? It's not up to us, the middle class, to pronounce on what's right and wrong for somebody who doesn't have the choices that we have. That's my personal view. Anyway, the long and the short of it is that it's been an exceptionally good stock for me.

INVESTOR TIPS

After 30 years in the fund management business, Round considers that the best approach for investors is to keep it simple and use their own experiences as investment ideas.

She says: "Keep your eyes open when you're out and about. Nothing is better than looking around you. If you go shopping, what shops are busy? Where are people going? That way you can see what businesses are doing well."

Round once took the benefit of her own advice on an investment in Kwik Fit.

"There was one near me and it was always busy so I thought it must be doing something right. It prompted me to look at it and I bought it for the fund."

Due diligence is also important for Round, as well as sticking to the hard facts and not getting distracted when the market is creating noise around certain stocks or events.

"If you're investing for 10 or 15 years, one quarter's earnings shouldn't make too much difference, even if the level of activity that you see around the shares is mad," she says. "You can't always pick the bottom and the top. If you think you can, you're a fool."

For this reason, regular saving is the best way to mitigate the ups and downs of the stock market, she recommends.

Above all, Round's philosophy focuses on "keeping it simple". She notes: "If you don't understand it, or it can't be explained to you in less than a third of a page, there's something not quite right."

Chapter 9

Britain's Warren Buffet?

Neil Woodford interviewed by Lawrence Gosling

Having enjoyed 26 successful years at Invesco Perpetual running its Income and High Income funds, Woodford left in 2013 to found his own investment fund management business, Woodford Investment Management, launching in June 2014, with the Woodford Equity Income fund. In 2013 he was awarded a CBE for services to the financial industry.

Lawrence Gosling: Who are the people you feel were your inspiration over the years?

Neil Woodford: First and foremost as an investment professional, the person who stands out as somebody who set a benchmark I wanted to emulate was Warren Buffett. I think his approach, his ability to communicate clearly, is just an extremely good lesson for the entire industry. Not just in terms of how he looks at investment and how he focuses on fundamentals and value, but also his openness in the way he communicates with investors is exemplary. He has been somebody that I have looked up to and admired.

LG: How early on in your career were you struck by him?

NW: I suppose I became more aware of him as a leading character in the industry about 20 years ago. In the past I used extracts from his letters to investors to sit in front of companies and say, "This is how you should think about, for example, share buybacks". The gospel according to Warren really has been the exemplar in a number of different situations.

In terms of how I have been framed as a fund manager, I wouldn't say that any one fund manager has stood out as somebody who taught me a lot. But Stephen Whittaker, who I worked with for 10 years [at Perpetual] was an important influence on me. I learned a lot from him and he is a very smart investor. And I think I learned also from my early experience at Perpetual what my purpose was really.

I think a lot of fund managers get completely lost in the weeds of the business and the industry and they lose sight of their socially useful purpose. I was made very aware of that very early. When I started to work for Perpetual, it was part of my routine to regularly stand up in front of large audiences of investors, not IFAs but investors, and talk to them about what I was doing with their money. That helped frame my perspective on what I needed to do, what investors expected me to do and what I felt I ought to deliver to them.

LG: Was that a bit of a surprise?

NW: Yes. But it didn't come as a surprise because that is what

I wanted to do. I left reasonably good career prospects at Eagle Star (in 1988) to go to a tiny little fund management business based in Henley-on-Thames. Nobody had ever heard of it. The industry was still reeling from the 1987 meltdown, and people who knew me thought I was mad.

But I knew what I really wanted as a fund manager; I didn't want to be part of a committee, making index-orientated investment decisions for institutional portfolios. It was just mush to me. I wanted to express my investment skill-set in a retail fund where if I succeeded or failed, it was very obvious. I wanted that – not that I wanted the limelight but I wanted to be able to express my investment skills unencumbered by committees and infrastructure. That is what attracted me to Perpetual. So when I got there and then was exposed to the end investor, it was what I wanted. It was what I set out to do.

LG: Is that why you never look at benchmarks?

NW: When I met my investor audience early on, it was clear to me that they had taken a pretty brave decision. They had taken money out of a secure building society deposit account and given it to me to manage in a fund. They had a return expectation. They didn't care what the index did and they certainly didn't think you had done a good job for them if the index was down 12% and you were down 10%. They had lost 10%. That was not a good outcome for them because they expected gains.

So my absolute return perspective was framed by how I wanted to run money, how I didn't want to be encumbered by committees and groups of people huddling around a consensus. I wanted to express my investment management talent. I believed that I had a skill set, but also I wanted to do that with a clear understanding of what my investors expected of me. And all of that clearly led to the starting point which is you don't start with the index. You start with: "What is the portfolio that I can construct that will sit within what I am allowed to own, that will deliver the appropriate risk-adjusted return to investors?" The framework was set by that ambition of long-term patient capital investment being driven by fundamentals, macro and corporate fundamentals. All of that flows naturally from that set of assumptions.

LG: How have you coped with the difference in investing time horizons over the period?

NW: I have always had a long-term perspective. My average holding period was typically always about 10 years at Perpetual and sometimes it stretched out way beyond that. Long-term discipline is what drives me. When I buy a share, rather like Buffett, I expect to be owning it forever. I don't have some exit event in mind when I buy a share. I have an ambition to participate in the growth of that business and the success of that business. The exit event is not something that I anticipate when I invest. And that applies from early-stage businesses all the way up to large businesses.

So yes, my investment horizon has always been long term. I have always had that three- to five-year vision. That is what I try and embed in my investment decision-making process. But typically my average holding period extends way beyond that.

LG: What about some periods when we have seen big dips in the market? Over the years, have you adapted your style? Do you see some of those dips as a big buying opportunity?

NW: Well typically I have been a fully-invested investor. Market dips are only a buying opportunity to the extent that you enjoy a cash flow. And at the moment, we do enjoy a cash flow so we did take advantage of the dip in the market to put some money to work, as it was coming in. But I don't try and anticipate market volatility.

I have always felt that the portfolio that I can invest in would always be able to do better than cash. So cash really has had no place in my portfolio. Clearly from time to time cash has appeared in the portfolio; if you are holding a large stock and it gets bid for and you get cash, then cash momentarily appears on the portfolio. But it pretty rapidly gets deployed. Because again, what are my return expectations for the portfolio? Are they in excess of cash? If they weren't I would be telling my investors to take their money away.

Those short-term market corrections are never really the buying opportunities that people talk about. But the other point you made about short-term underperformance; you have just got to think, if you have that long-term vision and you have a strategy, and you are not being buffeted by the next bit of news or the next quarterly profit announcement, or whatever it is, if you have a vision that sees through all that

123

volatility, you don't get led by the market. You get led by investment discipline. And that is an important differentiating thing. So short-term volatility is something you just navigate.

LG: It is presumably a lot easier for you to hold your nerve now when you are having periods of underperformance than it was 15 or 20 years ago?

NW: I am absolutely being held to account by my clients. If I don't deliver the investment outcomes that I have led them to expect, then I deserve to be sacked. My view has always been that my investment process is driven by what I think is in the best interests of my investors on a three- to five-year time horizon. At times, that will mean that I am very different from the stock market, and I have an obligation to communicate exactly why. So you don't park the portfolio and put your fingers in your ears and wake up in five years. You have an obligation, and I think I learnt this through the (late 1990s) tech bubble which was a painful period for me. There was a huge amount of pressure on me to change tack, to break my investment discipline, to buy into what the market was doing. I felt that the market had gone mad.

I questioned my own sanity from time to time during that period but I always came back to my investment discipline; what does my investment discipline, which has served me well in the past, tell me now? And every time I tested it, it gave me the same answer. So I didn't succumb but equally what happened to the late Tony Dye [the Phillips & Drew fund manager who resisted the rush to invest in tech and telecoms in the late 1990s and got sacked a month before the March 2000 crash] could have happened to me. I could have been fired. The business that employed me could have lost patience with me and fired me. But that would have happened before I compromised my investment discipline.

LG: So when you've been through those periods where the market is going against you and you're going back over the thesis, what were you asking yourself?

NW: It would be wrong to draw the analogy too closely, but there are some laws of the universe, the laws of physics and chemistry. And equally there are laws in the world of investment, and the fundamentals of valuation are, to my mind, laws.

Now they flex over time but as long as you revisit those laws, revisit your hypothesis, and if it adheres to those laws and you get the same result, then it is perfectly acceptable to say "this is my investment discipline, this is what guides my investment discipline, this is my approach, and my approach leads me to believe this".

If the market is doing something completely different, I think it's for your clients to make their minds up about whether you've completely taken leave of your senses or whether what you say makes sense. Ultimately it's your clients that make that judgement.

During that tech bubble, my clients did make a judgement which was, I think, that they suspected it was a bubble, they suspected that what was happening was pretty crazy, with a lot of very smart people sucked into it. But my investment discipline kept me away from it and I think most of my clients recognised that and backed me through that very difficult period. I'm not saying they would have carried on backing me for years but I would say over a one- to two-year period, the clients were pretty steadfast.

LG: Do you think you might have a longer period of grace now because you are 30 years down the line as opposed to 15 or 20?

NW: I don't know. You would hope that as long as what you said made sense, and it was consistent with what you said before, then I think investors are pretty patient. I think they are much less volatile than all the advisers that sit around the industry and they are much better informed than they used to be. They are more patient and I think you earn their trust over a period of time but you don't take it for granted.

I wouldn't want to rely on the fact that because I had done well in the past, that my investors would always sit through awful periods. I think you would have to earn their trust again. It would be a tough test.

LG: Do you think your style, your way of investing, would work in another geography?

NW: I am a big believer in knowing my limitations and sticking to the knitting. I am on a steep learning curve, more than 30 years into my career. That's what's intriguing and exciting and interesting about the job. That's why I really enjoy doing it. To believe that I could pick that skill set up and export it to a completely different geography – I just wouldn't feel comfortable with it.

LG: That leads on to what is the motivation after all this time?

NW: I have been doing this for a long time but I feel really invigorated by what's happened to me (since we launched Woodford Investment Management). It's been like a rebirth. I feel like I've rebooted my career. I am very excited about what we can achieve.

LG: Is that because you've got away from the corporate structure of a big parent?

NW: To some extent, yes. It's liberating. We've created something fit for purpose, fit for the 21st century. We've structured a business. We've had the luxury of having a clean sheet of paper and saying 'if you were going to build a fund management how would you build it?' And we think we've built that. And that's very exciting.

LG: Does that liberation include being able to avoid appearing in front of Parliamentary select committees in the future?

NW: I'm not saying I wouldn't ever do that. I see that as part of my activist agenda really. It's my responsibility as a fund manager to protect and represent the interests of my investors, and sometimes that means you actually go and try to change hearts and minds about things. That's part of fund management in my view.

LG: Do you consider yourselves to be a boutique?

NW: No, no, no. My mum used to work in a boutique. And it was a pretty small squishy little shop. So that's what I think about boutiques.

LG: But boutique asset management allows managers to focus on a niche group of investors?

NW: My world is retail fund management. The mass market, not ultra-high net worth. I'm focused on building a business that does a good job for the mass market and there's absolutely a need for it. I think there's an opportunity to marry a skill set with a need and I think we can do that at scale. We've got a serious piece of infrastructure. We have an ambition to build a serious fund manager business that does a good job.

LG: Do you think the fact that you come from a fairly normal upbringing has maybe unconsciously shaped or defined where you've gone?

NW: In part yes. I haven't got a chip on my shoulder or anything like that. We all go through slightly revolutionary phases in our life; I can remember mine at university. [laughter] I just thought Karl Marx made a lot of sense. We had a particularly good lecturer who was a Marxist economist and he was just very engaging. So you go through all that stuff but I haven't gone through my professional life with a chip on my shoulder about anything really. I just love what I do and I have been fortunate enough to find myself in a business where not only do I enjoy it but I have a reasonable talent for it. And that's an immense privilege.

LG: Do you in some way enjoy pitting your wits against the market, for want of a better expression?

NW: Yes, I think as you get older you get a bit more insight into your motivation, your personality, don't you? I think I'm a very competitive bloke. The way I am wasn't necessarily framed by my normal upbringing, I think it was framed by just being competitive.

But as I've got older, I've begun to realise it's something of an unfair fight because I think the market is structurally geared to make so many mistakes. There are so many opportunities to exploit. So I wouldn't for a moment pretend that I am brighter or better at being a fund manager than anybody else. I just think I am set up in a way that enables me to exploit anomalies the market creates because it is so driven by a short-term obsession.

LG: And is it becoming more anomalous, less efficient over time?

NW: Maybe the tech bubble was the pinnacle of inefficiency.

It's going to be hard to replicate that sort of extreme example of madness in the stock market. But I think structurally and institutionally, the market is profoundly inefficient because of some of the things we were talking about earlier, the motivations, the distortions that impact fund management behaviour and investor behaviour, and indeed corporate behaviour.

It's not just fund managers misallocating capital and being motivated by the wrong things. I think it's corporate, it's politics, it's capitalism, there's a pyramid of stuff that goes on to contribute to the distortions in the stock market. And my job is to exploit them.

LG: Is it becoming harder to see through that?

NW: It is tough. If I were to compare and contrast, one of the things that guided me through the tech bubble was a series in the FT of extracts from books that had been written about bubbles over history. The South Sea bubble, Tulip mania, there were a number of examples. They were fascinating and they helped me understand I wasn't going mad.

What they showed me was that the madness that occupied the market in '98, '99 and 2000, was extreme but in a way it was a repeat of what had happened in previous centuries. It's happened before and it will happen again. There are some things that remain constant, such as the propensity to have bubbles. And certainly in a world of zero interest rates and extraordinary monetary policy it's more likely that you'll have financial bubbles.

If I was to characterise investment now relative to when I started at Perpetual, I would say that there is additional complexity now. There's regulatory, political and geographic complexity in a very much more connected world today than we had before. When I started, I didn't really have to worry about what was going on in Russia, it was behind the Iron Curtain. But now, Russian sanctions have had an impact on Rolls Royce's P&L.

The new dynamic of China and emerging economies, all these things are new and quite complex to read. But the reaction of a lot of fund managers is "it's all too bloody difficult; I'm just going to forget about macro and focus on picking companies". I think that's like looking at half a picture. To get a full sense of how good the artist is, you've got to look at the whole picture.

LG: Is it a bit of a cop-out?

NW: Yes, I think it is. Every company that I have ever sat in front of, they will always say there are some things that we can control, our P&L, our balance sheet, our cash flow, our capital deployment, our strategy, but there are also the things that we can't control. To ignore the things that you can't control because it's all too difficult seems to me to be an abrogation. In forming a view about how well companies will perform in future, you've got to have a macro perspective. Macro is really important; it always has been. Sometimes it is quite stable. There were periods in the '90s when it was very stable in the UK. There was a period of relatively benign macroeconomics when inflation was coming down, interest rates were coming down.

But during that period, there was some macro volatility. Things happened. There was an Asian bubble in 1998. There were wars. But broadly it was quite a stable period. But there are, equally, times of great volatility and I think we are in a more volatile period now. I think it is incumbent on fund managers to think about it and think about how it impacts your stock selection.

LG: How do you differentiate?

NW: Not everything is relevant. It may be profoundly important from a geopolitical point of view but it may not be important economically. What is happening in Syria arguably is unbelievably disturbing geopolitically, but from a macroeconomic point of view it's hard to see what the impact is.

So I'm not saying that I react to everything or impute importance to things that are not important; I'm trying to focus on what really is, macroeconomically, very important.

LG: So low interest rates, monetary policy …?

NW: Yes, extraordinary monetary policy. What's driving it? What I'm preoccupied by … is whether we are enduring a period of secular stagnation. What is driving secular stagnation? Why are developed economies not responding in a conventional way to the most unbelievable set of monetary and fiscal policy stimuli? What is stopping the developed world responding in the way that central banks anticipated that they would?

Central bank models are breaking down; they are not explaining what is going on in the economy. It's quite easy for central bankers to look ludicrous these days because they just keep getting everything wrong. And the reason they are getting it wrong is because the economy is not responding. So I don't think they have diagnosed the problem properly yet. You can't possibly help a patient if you don't diagnose their illness properly. I think the same for the economy.

LG: And is that because it's "an illness" none of them have ever seen before?

NW: Arguably yes. We are in uncharted territory. This is new; there is no guidebook for this. They are sort of making it up as they go along. And so I think that's really important. But also what's going on in China, the shift in the Chinese economic model from infrastructure-led growth to consumption-led growth. Currency wars; what's happening to commodity prices; how trade surpluses play out and how those dictate where currencies go. All of these are things I think about when I'm thinking about how a company is going to perform today, tomorrow and in three- to five-years' time. It's my job to impute all the things that are relevant to stock selection into my stock collection.

LG: So why don't you see this as a pressure? How do you cope, managing the money that you do?

NW: It's a bit of a boiled frog thing. You've been in a hot saucepan for a while and you have sort of got used to it. So I think there must be an element of that. I certainly don't believe my own PR. I know that I'm only as good as the next period of performance. I know that the expectation is there but ultimately how I perform in the future will be the judge of how well this business performs, how successful we are.

And it's a tough, competitive environment; it's unpredictable; there's lots of uncertainty around. But I find I really enjoy the whole process of thinking through portfolio construction. What are the things that are relevant to it? Corporate fundamentals, macro fundamentals, how they interplay.

That's what I find really interesting. It's an important part of trying to frame my understanding of where we are, where we're likely to be. All this stuff that I distil down to an interest rate view, a growth view, an inflation view, a deflation view.

LG: So what else do you read, where else do you get your ideas from?

NW: We get an enormous amount of information thrown at us. It's hard, that's probably the most frustrating thing about what I do. You've just got to keep kissing loads of frogs or diving for pearls. I sometimes get 300 emails a day, so maybe 5% might be worth reading. You don't know at the start of the day which

5% you are going to be interested in. You might have a hunch that you want to look at this or look at that.

Not all of your day is dictated by the newsflow but some of my day is dictated by the new information that is produced globally that may impact what I have already assumed. So when you model your view it's dynamic. And it has to be tuned constantly by new information. So your investment antennae are absorbing new information all the time and slightly adjusting your model based on that new information. Sometimes there's no adjustment, sometimes there's a lot.

LG: Presumably there's a group of people in and around the market who you've always felt that you've got good information and good ideas from?

NW: Our investment inputs, our investment antennae are always twitching. We're out there receiving huge amounts of information; some comes in from trusted sources; I read the FT religiously. I have great relationships with analysts and strategists and economists and sales guys. And then every now and then, we will establish a new relationship based on one piece of research. Increasingly now we are fragmenting our research spend to encompass research analysts that are outside conventional investment banking businesses.

LG: What's the most unusual place you can remember getting an idea from that developed into something you put into a portfolio?

NW: I couldn't give you an eyebrow anecdote. But what tends to happen is there's the conventional investment universe – and we've got some very interesting holdings in that universe – but we've also got a whole portfolio of early-stage investments, quoted and unquoted.

The way those ideas have come to us is quite interesting. Some of them have come from personal relationships, personal friends. Some have come because somebody else heard that we were prepared to fund early-stage businesses. For instance, we've invested in a business that's got new flushing toilet technology. It saves 80% of the flush. So there's stuff like that. These ideas have come to us because people have heard that we fund new technology. So they've rung me up, they've sent me an email, and sometimes I open the attachment, I read the email, I think no, I don't like that, and sometimes I go, "wow, this is really interesting". And then we get them in and next thing you know, three months later we've made an investment. So it's not predictable.

LG: The best and worst investments over the last 30 years?

NW: Oh, God, you miss so many. Frankly I've just lost count. There are so many things that you miss. That's something that you have to accept as a fund manager. When I first started running money, I thought my goal was to build a portfolio that had within it the best performing stocks in the stock market in any one period of time. Better than anything else. It was a sort of maximising discipline that I was pursuing. It was ludicrous.

I very early, very quickly learnt that that was a very, very dangerous pursuit.

So I quite quickly learnt that my investors wanted an outcome and there were many other portfolios that could deliver that outcome, I just hoped that I could construct one of them. So I optimised in my approach and satisfied myself that I would leave it to others to deliver the sort of blow-out. I would just concentrate on my clients getting rich slowly, rather than very quickly.

I've not been preoccupied by things that have been brilliant or things that have been less than brilliant. I know I've missed loads of great things, but I know I've missed some real horror shows as well through good investment discipline. I've protected investors' capital mostly by what I haven't owned rather than what I have owned.

I think some of the best investments I've ever made are the ones I've got in the portfolio now. I think that we've got some investments that could genuinely change the world. They're tiny now but they could be genuinely gigantic. There are a couple of early-stage tech businesses.

LG: You've always been interested in this, haven't you?

NW: Well what fascinates me is that they look like fantastic investment opportunities. The reason I own them is because I look at them through the same lens that I look at the likes of BAT. I am looking for undervalued assets. And undervalued assets come in all shapes and sizes. My view is that these are profoundly undervalued assets.

Just to give the background, the UK for centuries has been the cradle of science and technology and innovation. But more recently, certainly in the 20th century and the early 21st century, we have led the world – in graphene, human genome, gene sequencing, cancer, devices. The largest selling drug in the world, Humira, was invented by Cambridge Antibody, which was a UK business that AstraZeneca bought.

We've got a track record in the UK of brilliant innovation and invention but we're lamentable at converting that into successful businesses that employ people, pay taxes and grow the economy. Most of our successful innovation has created economic value abroad rather than at home.

And to my mind, that continues to create an opportunity. We are carrying on innovating, we have got four of the best universities in the world, top 10 universities in the world, within spitting distance of where we're sitting now; UCL, Imperial College, Cambridge and Oxford. Unbelievable scientific leadership, and nobody wants to provide any capital apart from a few weird investors like me. I think there's a massive opportunity there.

Chapter 10

The Very British Activist Investor

Richard Buxton interviewed by Lawrence Gosling

Richard Buxton joined Old Mutual as Head of UK Equities in June 2013 after he made his name during the 10 years he spent at Schroders, where he managed the Schroders UK Alpha Plus fund and earned a reputation for being an outspoken "activist" investor of the type more normally seen in the US. He took to a life in the City of London just on the cusp of the Big Bang in the late '80s, first with Brown Shipley Asset Management and then with Barings in the early '90s. He says an arts degree should be no hindrance for anyone wishing to join the investment world, suggesting fund management is as much an art as it is a science. In the summer of 2015 he became CEO of Old Mutual Global Investors.

Lawrence Gosling: Most people tell me they stumbled into fund management?

Richard Buxton: Yes, very much. I stumbled along to the milk round in the third year of university, having previously thought I could become an academic or teach. There were merchant banks and stockbrokers and partly the reason I went there was that the only bit of the economics and politics A-level I'd done that had really fascinated me, was on the stock market. The idea that you could buy and sell bits of paper and make money.

I went along, completely in the dark, and ended up beginning to work out what the difference between a stockbroker and a merchant banker was; do you particularly want to be a stockbroker and therefore sell things, or do research into things, or do you want to be user of those services, run money, and that was definitely the route I wanted to go.

My father, 40 years a clearing banker, was horrified at the idea of my going to the City. He got me to go and apply for a job at the Bank of England because he thought at least that was sensible and respectable. My mother wanted me to be in the Civil Service which she'd done and she met such nice people there. So I got a job offer at the Bank of England and a job offer from Brown Shipley and there was no question as to which (I would choose).

You're thrown in at the deep end and haven't the faintest idea what anything means, and which way is up, and they started me on the bond department, [it was called the] gilt department, and I spent my first year grappling with trying to understand currencies and bond prices and things. I look back and (think) that was probably a very, very good thing because understanding what drives bond markets, the price of money, drives most things.

After a year I switched across to UK equities. I certainly got very good advice; like just go to anything, turn up to the opening of the envelope and just go to any company meeting, company lunch, it doesn't matter what sector, but just be like a sponge, absorb as much as you possibly can.

LG: Did you feel like it was good advice at the time?

RB: Yes. I did. Just be curious, just try and find out about stuff, what makes companies tick and what's different in different sectors. I started in 1985, so it was just pre-Big Bang though most alliances (and) marriages had already been set up, everyone had paired off. But you could still, just, under the aegis of a distinguished, extinct broking firm go on the floor of the Stock Exchange. A pretty amazing perspective of the old City and all that went with it.

LG: What was good and bad about the old City?

RB: Well, (then Prime Minister Margaret) Thatcher was absolutely right to break commissions and cartels and so on. I think some of the values were actually good; some less good. (The City) was a village. That's kind of nice, and to the extent that people still come here to meet the money and so companies will come and walk round. And I was still naive and inexperienced and learning on the job in ways that – now, I probably wouldn't get in, full stop.

You didn't then have to have formed an investment club when you were 14 and gone and saved an African village in your holidays and all that. You weren't competing with 2,000 people for two jobs. And you weren't then put through the

CFA (Chartered Financial Analyst) hell for three years so I genuinely would probably not have got it and/or got to the level of being able to do what I'm doing now.

I learnt with other people's money. You just kind of trained on a small fund and you learnt through your mistakes. The industry has professionalised (since) and you don't do that anymore, you go through understanding a bit more about capital markets and how to understand a company's P&L and balance sheet, and all that sort of stuff. But then it's curious that there is then a risk you produce all sorts of similar types of people. (But) this business is no science, it is an art.

Because it is about judging both management of companies you're investing in, and the mood of the market, the collective wisdom of everyone else out there trying to do the same thing. That's an art, it's not a science. It's why I'm convinced you get better at it the longer you do it, and experience counts. It's just possible that the changing nature of how people get into this and the increased professionalism of the industry, which on the one hand is laudable and you don't learn with someone else's money etc., but does it mean that you end up missing some of the people. Do you end up with a slightly skewed (intake)?

LG: When did you begin to feel like you were quite a competent investor? That you could be let loose with other people's money?

RB: I remember in my second year at Brown Shipley, when I'd moved on to the equity side, I was so confident that inflation was going to fall and interest rates were going to fall, that I took the entirety of the National Savings that my parents had given me when I was 21, £2,000, and put it on a gilt option. The senior guy on the equity side there, he dealt PA [personal account] quite a lot, and he said why are you doing this? And he put some PA money on it as well, and we trebled our money.

After the 1987 crash everyone was terrified. I was fairly confident that we were going to fall into a recession and it was going to be difficult. I left Brown Shipley in 1988 and went back to Oxford to see if I did want to still be an academic and do a further degree. But I did that for one year and whilst I thoroughly enjoyed it, I kept in touch with the market, with my chums in the City, and I knew that I wanted to go back. I moved to Barings in 1990 as a UK equity manager. Within a year they'd had a restructuring there. I was bunged into client services.

I wasn't stock picking for a good few years. I did – okay. I actually got involved in asset allocation, ended up on the global strategy committee. It was only post Barings/Leeson that the opportunity arose to come back into the UK equity stock picking and I picked up the Baring UK Growth Fund. We were down £10m in my first few weeks through redemptions and I built and worked and said, "Just watch this". I ran that for a further six years and it was top quartile and triple A-rated and we had £330m. By then I started to think "I could do this", but the classic danger of being a young fund manager is you're in the office every day, so you've got to do something every day. So you just take profits and you sell things that actually you want for the long term.

I moved to Schroders in 2001 to manage higher-performance pension funds, and persuaded them eventually that I had a following in the retail market and it would be worth running a retail fund. I designed that to focus on those stocks I think where I have conviction that they'll make money. I actually did think the market was going to go sideways for 10 to 15 years from 2000/2001, and therefore there'd be absolutely no point in sticking close to the index. You want to differentiate. So I designed that which I still run, effectively.

LG: How does a fund manager design a strategy for a fund?

RB: I had a macro view of where the market was going, therefore I didn't want to build the portfolio in relation to the index. I wanted to abandon tracking error and all that constraint. Then it was well, genuinely, how many good ideas do you have? I reckon about 30 to 35, and the rest is slightly less good ideas. With 35 stocks, you can hopefully have enough things where you can nurture.

When I talked to Schroders, initially, they were not really very keen. But I didn't take no for an answer and got support from the people who had hired me to do the pension fund and I just very determinedly said, "This is what I want to do and how I want to run money."

In the early couple of years, I was higher turnover still because I just felt it was so important to build the early track record that I was actually taking profit because it was a small

144

fund and so you can do that. It had always had the FTSE bias and that again was in all honesty because the Barings fund I'd had was predominantly FTSE and mid-cap and then some small caps, some of which did phenomenally well and some of which, classically, imploded.

I do realise that actually small cap is a very different game. There are so many of them, it's massively labour-intensive. I'm quite lazy, and you really have got a lot of people involved and really (have to) get to meet the companies, a zillion times a year.

LG: So what makes a good company for you?

RB: There's going to be different things in there and you want different things in there. You want different drivers. And of course like everyone else, if you can find the new management self-help recovery story, then particularly being patient you can make a lot of money out of things like that. Or things where it's partly self-help and partly economic recovery and so on. I guess you need good people around you, I would always say that. I can't do this on my own; I've got to have good people around me. They're probably doing detailed fundamental analysis in ways that I'm not, I'm piggy-backing off their perceptions and insights and knowledge. I am a classic generalist fund manager, mile-wide inch-deep knowledge.

LG: Let's talk about the management. What impresses you?

RB: I think it's honesty and if you're a long-term investor you're going to see these people a lot and you're going to build up a picture over time and to some extent. We know that contracts slip, we know that the world changes and you have to tweak the strategy. But it's how people deal with that and how they can talk about how they're adapting and so on and that you can see that it makes sense, there is a return coming at the end of this investment phase, or whatever.

The old Buffett things; that by the time you get to be CEO you're not short of self-belief and confidence and so on, but if you can have degrees of humility, or acknowledgement when things do go a bit wrong.

LG: Is there anything very subjective about their appearance?

RB: You do notice. Waistcoats. Waistcoats with lapels. People who insist on their title; Doctor so-and-so, or Sir, Professor. People who insist on that, it's usually a bad sign that they've got some sort of ego issue. There've been several companies where it's ended in tears, people that have insisted on their title.

LG: How easy is it to be patient as an investor?

RB: In a way you couldn't run the amount of money we do if you were frenetic, unless you had a totally different diversified thing. How easy is it to be patient? You're very alive to performance and when you're struggling, and you keep going over the things that are hurting you and you spend time dwelling on that, meeting the companies again. Not I guess when one's been doing it long enough, you accept that in the short term share prices ping around all over the place and it's a nonsense, or not something to be fazed by, and it's the great Buffett quote: "In the short term, the market's a voting machine and in the long run it's a weighing machine". It's about accumulating mass over time and not worrying about the short-term votes. There are more short-term operators driving share prices, for sure. But actually that should logically provide opportunities for the longer-term.

LG: Do you feel under more pressure now being at OMGI, having been very successful at Schroders?

RB: Well if there's any pressure it is pressure I wanted to take. I felt I had another big job in me. Eleven years at Barings, 12 at Schroders, one more. Can he do it again? Can you demonstrate that you can do it again with some of the same people and some different people? And a different environment. The appeal of being somewhere smaller and really making a difference was attractive.

And do I feel some pressure? Yes, particularly to the team who have come to join me on this journey because they've just placed a huge amount of trust in you and they've got kids and families and school fees, and we've got to make this work. So yes, I feel that but it's not something I wear on a daily basis. Do I worry when I'm on holiday? Not a thing. Don't have a BlackBerry, don't read the newspaper. I know a lot of fund managers who just can't bear not being in touch. I don't need to do that at all. So am I sitting here worrying about stuff? No. It's just there.

LG:. How do you explain the value of active management?

RB: Four percent per annum, outperformance since the launch of the Schroder fund, net of fees, is the simple answer. The likes of Nick Train [Lindsell Train], Nigel Thomas [of AXA Framlington], none of us are going to get it right every year because we can't. But you shut your eyes and back these people for three, five, 10 years and they'll do better than passive.

LG: When you are asked about people in the City being overpaid, how do you respond?

RB: I think income inequality is a big issue in the UK. I really do think it is an issue. I feel that I do a job that is worthwhile. Not only from the point of view of I'm trying to protect and grow the value of people's savings, I wish there were more people at the low end of the income bracket that were saving and getting the benefits of this, that's another whole issue, the fact that you're just making wealthy people wealthier.

But equally, through active management in a way you can't through passive, (we can) try and improve corporate performance, try and get the right board structures, the right calibre of people, the right incentive structures.

But I do think wealth inequality, income inequality, is a real issue that is beginning to break the social pact, the trust that means that a society can function. I worry about that.

LG: Activism, particularly US-based activism, is often seen as nasty and horrible. There is a more positive turn to it now?

RB: Yes, engaging with companies. I still think the US, because their corporate structure is so different, it means a lot of US activist investors have to go via proxy votes, via board battles – we all know America is a litigious society. Whereas in the UK you don't have to do that. We're all terribly British and just have a nice cup of tea with someone.

I think in the UK, we cleaned up our act post-Maxwell, Polly Peck, and all that stuff. We've evolved the governance. Come 2000, it was Enron and it was the US that fell off. We didn't have anything in the 2000 bust that was really scandalous. I think the investing institutions have continued to, at varying paces, recognise the value of gentle activism, of engaging on issues of pay, incentives, checks and balances, etc.

LG: Is it harder to change some companies such as the banks as an external investor than it perhaps is a business like Tesco?

RB: Yes, the bigger the company the harder it is to change because the more diversified the share register – without doubt. And banks in particular, they've got the regulators all over them and this never-ending journey to the Promised Land. But it was impossible to effect change at RBS until too late. I think that is true of any large company if there is a degree of intransigence and a kind of, well, divide and rule affecting the shareholder base. It's always going to be easier if it's a company where there are three or four key investors who own quite a lot.

At Schroders we were always trying to do things quietly behind closed doors, but if we weren't getting anywhere, I was prepared to be an arsehole and go public. I didn't actually enjoy it, I don't get a kick out of doing this but it's amazing the incoming emails and phone calls we get from people supporting us.

But it has meant that I still punch above my weight in terms of pure FuM because I'm sure that some companies or their advisers go, "Well, you'd probably better go and see him and talk to Richard, probably worth keeping him onside because you just don't want him mouthing off". So being prepared to go public – I've got the scars from a few battles and of course you're never going to get everything right – but at least trying to do the right thing. And as I say, you get some interesting feedback from investors.

LG: Would it be right to say you're proud of what you do as a fund manager?

RB: Yes, I am. I derive satisfaction from it. In the sense that you're only as good as your last game and you've got to keep delivering, but I am proud and I'm pleased with some of the corporate battles that we've fought. Such as when Stuart Rose was made executive chair of M&S in complete breach of Cadbury Code best practice. If a household name like M&S

did it and got away with it, every other company would go well, we'll just tear Cadbury up.

And it was the principle. David Michels, the ex-hotelier who was the deputy chairman of M&S at the time, said to me, "Well, you've lost the battle but you've won the war." I think that is a point of principle that was worth defending.

LG: Is it as simple as saying history repeats itself in the markets?

RB: We have the conversations around the desk about does this feel a bit like 1998, or that sort of thing. It's just a reference point for sets of circumstances. It does help you form your judgement as to where you think we are now in the cycle, such as it exists.

LG: Are there books that maybe have had an influence on you?

RB: The book that I have given numerous copies away to younger people when they come into the industry is *The Money Game*, by 'Adam Smith', written in the '60s under a pseudonym by a money manager at that time. All the stock names are clearly completely different and so on but that in terms of behaviour, the guy says this is a kids' market and we're not giving a portfolio to kids who have no history and infinite belief. And it's just the right time to take it back from the kids. And it's brilliant, absolutely brilliant.

But I think there's been a lot of looking back through

history and every cycle, every generation has its shell companies, are going to go and do this, and the things that go up like a rocket and come down like a stick and I think virtually every decade there's been a brand new super-smart entrant to the insurance market. And they just start taking premium and it's only later that you get the cheques going out. And then independent insurers: there was one in the '70s, there was definitely one in the '80s.

And finally the great George Blakey book on the history of the London stock market since 1945, just going through what the economy was doing, then some of the key stocks, absolutely fascinating.

Chapter 11

The Difference between
Investing and Gambling

James Henderson interviewed by Lawrence Gosling

James Henderson joined the firm which bears the same name back in 1983, after completing one year as a trainee accountant. He was appointed manager of the Lowland Investment Trust in 1990, a trust which he still runs. Since 2005 he has also been the manager of the firm's UK Equity income fund, alongside the Henderson Opportunities investment trust which he took on sole responsibility for in 2003. Henderson is a regular racegoer, and he says that investors can learn from the gambling world about probabilities and the pricing up of risk.

Lawrence Gosling: Can we talk first about your early days in fund management and how you came about deciding on an investment style?

James Henderson: I had been Richard Smith's assistant in the late 1980s [then manager of Lowland], and I'd seen how he had been running it. So when I took it on in 1990, I went away and tried to think what had worked. It had been very successful for Richard in the '80s, and I thought about what I might do differently. And actually there's very little that I think I do differently to how it was run then.

Being an income fund in those days, it was mildly contrarian. You were always buying things that were out of fashion – usually out of fashion – and that's what put them on a high yield. You were focusing on cash generation because cash pays dividends and you kept away from things that were in fashion and low yielding. That helps point you, I think, in the right direction.

I think perhaps over time I've modified that a bit in that I'm not quite so dogmatic on yield as I was and the reason for that is that things do change. I think now the income story is quite well trodden around. In those days it was less so.

LG: Why is that?

JH: It's partly that the fund flows have been into that area, so it's made income investing less of a contrarian view. I like to think that I remain a value-orientated investor, but sometimes value can be in zero-yielding. I went to presentations a few years ago and would listen to other people and they would tell you about companies with strong balance sheets, generating cash with really strong business franchises, and cash in their balance sheet, and you sort of knew a contrarian would think perhaps the area to invest in was the more challenged companies, those fighting for their role in life because they had a lot of debt. And actually over the last five years, you would have done better in those companies where they've actually been sorting problems out. Often they cut their dividend at the time. So that was where the contrarian trade was. Sometimes I'm now buying zero yielders because that is the area that is being neglected.

What I tried to do from the start was rather a multi-cap approach. There are no big calls on markets or big calls on macroeconomics. What I'm trying to do is pay attention to things that people aren't paying so much attention to, and that way I think you can add value over time. There are so many things too difficult for me to understand, so I don't build anything round it. I just hope that the companies we invest in will deal with whatever is thrown at them because the managements are strong, even if they are not perceived to be that good a management at the time.

LG: Is that the benefit of experience?

JH: I suppose I've watched the big macro investors and I've admired them when they get it right but often people get it right for a bit and then get it wrong. There are so many variables in your big macro calls and events will come along and have a leftfield input to the tidiest macro call and you get it wrong. I think it is very difficult to run money like that.

You're more likely to be able to add value if you pay attention to a company that no one else is paying attention to, and only a few people are following. You're more likely to spot that actually it's going better than the general market might perceive it to be. They might think it's too small, they might think it's in the wrong industry, they might think that the management team has missed opportunities, when actually the management team hasn't: it's just that events transpired for that management team to look as though they've missed opportunities.

I wouldn't say this normally, but actually I've also watched how gamblers gamble. I've always enjoyed racing, watching gamblers, and I knew a friend, and always on Derby Day, he used to go to Newcastle races. Everyone thinks on Derby Day about Epsom and who is going to win the Derby. There are 30 runners in the Derby, and everyone is trying to win it and it's very, very competitive and very, very difficult. But if everyone is paying attention to the Derby, there's a chance that something is mispriced at another meeting.

If you can keep backing at 5-1 horses that should be 5-2, you will make a good living over time. And it's nothing to do with conviction – it's really to do with probabilities. If you can find value, you can have a bet at 5-1 when it should be 5-2, you will over time get a decent return. And that's always been behind how I invest.

You have to be careful because it is investing; it is about companies and another thing a good gambler might do is they always say that a win a day keeps the bailiff away. In other words, don't get greedy, nothing goes on forever. So you've got to be disciplined and not greedy. And also, the other side of that is if you don't get greedy, you shouldn't get overly careful. At the end of the day, it isn't life and death. So don't get the emotional swings; you see them most intensely with gamblers but really the good gambler, again, doesn't have those swings.

But on the other hand you shouldn't have a bet unless it's enough for it to hurt when you lose. Otherwise you're probably just donating to the bookie's holiday fund. Because it's got to matter and I try and bring that a little bit to the portfolio. Every investment I make it needs to matter. So you can't just dabble at it or you shouldn't be doing it. We were talking about people who make very few investments, they do matter and I might run much longer lists but then I'm often dealing in more challenged companies. So actually a small amount in a challenged company actually matters to me as much as having a large stake in a quality company because of the potential downside involved.

LG: Do you still describe yourself as a contrarian?

JH: Yes. I would be careful about these sorts of conversations. Early on, I was struggling and I was trying to articulate value investing, being a contrarian. To put a racing point in, Johnny Henderson, who was trainer Nicky Henderson's father, said to me, "Don't worry about value and all that, just buy a few shares before they go up, and everyone will be happy with you". And that's at the end of the day what I still think about. We can overcomplicate the business, we can worry about these badges and everything else – and we can worry about falling in love with an idea – but actually all our job really is, at the end of the day, about these stocks and whether they go up. That's my reality check.

What do I mean by contrarian? I mean it's the opposite of momentum actually. And momentum investing can work well.

They spot a trend, and they play on that trend. Every trend gets taken too far somewhere out there, so there is a relative contrarian investor, and good momentum investors can get good returns and good contrarian investors can get good returns, and vice versa. So you are buying the more unloved businesses, the ones the momentum guy has given up on. What I found out when I was battle tested – tested several times over the period I've run money – is I'm always buying too early and I'm always selling too early.

I try to mitigate doing that so at the moment I buy slower than I used to. Instead of buying a quarter of what I'm going to buy and then another quarter, I buy a tenth of what I'm going to buy. I buy slower and step it up as I become convinced that it's right to try and mitigate this buying too early. And the same with selling, I often sell too early, and again, I'm selling slower because there are momentum people out there that do take things and can be very successful investors. But that said, though I'm doing that, that's led to my list becoming longer because I'm taking longer to buy and longer to sell. But I am aware that usually in investing you make your next mistake trying to avoid your last one. So I have to be careful about that. That would be a slight change to my approach in recent years, to take a bit longer. You can definitely see that too often I've bought too early and it does sometimes hopefully come right in time, but it would have been better to have bought a bit later. The same with selling. Yes, things have gone up after I've sold them, maybe it would play itself out in time but it would have been better to time it better. So I'm working on that.

But what is contrarian investment? Partially there is an element of mean reversion in the markets, things going too much both ways and the contrarian is partially playing the mean reversion that is going on in the markets, and talking the opposite way to the way the momentum guys go.

LG: You seem to have an open mind about which parts of the market you invest in?

JH: That's absolutely right. I think if things change, you need to change a bit and I think what's coming out of our universities is now different than in the past, in terms of the ambition of the [university], the ambition of the founder, or the professor. So sometimes you talk to the professor, he's telling you about his ambition to float his company or something like that. That's a generalisation but there are a lot of academics that are producing very fine papers. But there are obviously a bit fewer. Certainly there are some professors with real ambition to take their idea, make it a commercial company, make it really happen and do the UK's balance of payments a lot of good.

So I see opportunities in that area which has been a difficult area in the past. I think, "This time, why is it different?" The funding is better in the UK than it was. It used to be a very difficult area to take companies to the next stage, so people often used to sell them quite early – on to Americans particularly. When you think of all the good things that have come out of the UK that have never been taken all the way, that would suggest that in the UK there are a lot of good ideas but we've failed in the past to take them to a commercial element. And that may just be changing. So that's a generalised view.

Actually in recent years I've been doing more research, and it always takes longer for an idea to reach a commercial point. If you come in after a round or two of funding, you might be in at a better time. Often by that stage there's less blue sky and you are actually going to see where the earnings are going to come from, rather than it just being a big concept.

AIM is a very good market for raising money for this type of company. I think AIM is where the next generation of really good UK businesses are going to be found. Lighter regulation is a good thing; obviously it can be abused sometimes, but actually lighter regulation, speed of access to investors to be able to raise money, and more flexibility are the reason that the young entrepreneur is attracted to AIM. The young entrepreneurs today, some of them are going to be running the successful companies of tomorrow.

LG: So if your starting point in general terms is looking at different parts of the market, and companies that not many other people are looking at, how do you then take that into those investment ideas?

JH: I just talked about start-ups. Those tech potentials, they'd be 5% of my portfolio. It wouldn't be more than that. The bulk of my money could be in more mainstream areas like industrial companies. For an industrial, to screen for value and to give me some ideas, I look at the turnover, the sales of the company and compare it to the enterprise value, i.e. the market cap adjusted for debt and pension deficits. So that way you get a feel for the size of a business and its sales. And the attraction of that number, when you're screening, is the sales number is a hard number and the market cap is a hard number, the debt at a point in time is a hard number. So you haven't got provisioning, you haven't got depreciation charges, you've got what would you pay for those sales.

With a good industrial company, it usually comes to £1 of sales to £1 of market cap, just a very rough guide. So if you can buy a company with good product at a quarter of sales, it's probably losing money at the time, or it's had some problem. But the question is, when you see that, why is that the case? And that can often be the starting point. In an industry, if you are at quarter of sales, I then look at are those sales and ask whether in time it is going to make a better margin on those sales. And you've got something to work with. So perhaps a new management team is going into that company, and it's got these sales, is it going to get a better margin on those sales? That's often an easier place to start from than, say, with a company that says it will double sales over the next five years. You've got the sales; you're going to bring the discipline to them and learn how to make a better margin on those sales.

LG: So simplistically, if a business just carries on doing what it's doing only more efficiently, any significant uptick in sales will be worth even more?

JH: Yes, exactly. I find that is a good discipline in the industrial arena. There's no screen that's going to get you away from doing the work of understanding the company. But as a screen for ideas, I find that very clean and simple. Then often there will be a good reason why it's a quarter of sales. It's got a perfectly good product but because of one thing or another, something's gone wrong – if the sales are robust enough these things can be put right with less risk perhaps than saying, "Oh, this company is going to double and then double sales again". These companies have already got the customers, they just need to either look after them better, charge them a bit more, or be more disciplined in their manufacturing process.

LG: What's the importance of generating yield?

JH: I think income is important, but to get income you need to grow the capital since the capital produces income. So everything I believe should grow, nothing should be there just for income because companies don't stand still, they're either going forward or they're going backwards. If you think something standing still but is giving you a nice income – you'll probably soon be declining. That's happening quicker and quicker because one of the things that changes is the life cycle of companies, it's getting shorter. This is partly because they're less asset rich. The speed of information flow is greater so the second and third best is under pressure quicker, and if you start to fail, it happens faster.

The classic case would be something like Tesco. When I started Tesco was the aggressive guy on the block: stack it high, sell it cheap. It became, as it matured, the key supermarket on the high street and beat all the others up really. But its period in the sun was fairly short and it's now in decline. It may be that it's relearning and coming back but the swifter cycle is happening across industries. And in that industry, you'd have thought it would take a bit longer because you've got the assets, you've got the place on the high street, but actually it's happening everywhere at speed.

So you have to be careful, I think, to believe that this is just a steady state and it'll keep producing income, because it won't. It needs first and foremost to be growing as a business. And once they stop growing as a business, even if the yield looks good, you have to be very careful about the investment. So the focus is grow the capital in companies that are growing and income discipline, mild income discipline, and that's where you get income growth over time. And it is income growth, that's why you own shares.

I think it's easy to produce higher income in the short term but if you do it at the expense of capital, you'll have less capital in time to produce it. And that we sometimes forget. What you're wanting is, in my view, you start with a low yield when companies are growing their dividend and the power of compounding kicks in over time and you get sustainable income growth.

LG: What makes you come into the office every day?

JH: Well I do like being paid, I need to be paid. But I enjoy it. I enjoy being competitive but I do enjoy watching the economy, I do find that interesting to observe.

Chapter 12

Dare to be Different

Helena Morrissey interviewed by Jane Wallace

Helena Morrissey has been chief executive at Newton Investment Management since 2001, having joined the firm in 1994 as a bond fund manager. She admits her rise to the top was as much of a surprise to her as anyone, but as founder of the Thirty Per Cent Club – which seeks to raise the participation of women across UK boardrooms – she is very much in favour of women taking up more top roles in the investment world. Her secondary school education was at a comprehensive school and she is a strong advocate of getting people from diverse backgrounds into financial markets.

Jane Wallace: You made your name as a bond fund manager. What was your big break?

Helena Morrissey: I was the junior of a two-woman bond desk at Newton. It was a very small part of the overall business and it was very difficult. I joined in February 1994 on practically the same day that the Fed started raising rates. And we had a pretty bad year.

At the end of it my colleague resigned. Stewart Newton, the then chief executive, said: "Don't worry, Helena. We'll appoint a guru over you who is much more senior," to which I said, "Well, while you look for that person, do you mind if I run the bond money?"

He was great about letting me do that but I would have to report to him on what I'd been doing every day at four o'clock in the afternoon. He was a great mentor and a great investor, but every six weeks or so he would move to another part of the business and I would have to go with him. So I was the butt of a few jokes because of that.

Of course, that was a tremendous learning experience. He was a big-picture investor and very good at spotting trends. So I always ran the money in that way. I wasn't really a typical bond investor, eking out a basis point here or there. I would take very big positions, which was unusual, but that was the way I'd learnt how to do it.

There were a couple of really big calls which I guess built my reputation as a credible person at Newton. One was around the time that the Labour Government was elected in 1997. Everyone was so scared about buying bonds because they thought Labour would let the deficit get out of control. I thought all of that was discounted so I stocked up on what seemed a very long-dated bond at the time. Bizarrely, of course, it matured in 2015. I remember it well. It was wrong for a quarter and then it was tremendous.

JW: How did you progress from there to being chief executive officer?

HM: When Mellon acquired Newton, I was one of four people running the investment strategy. We had an inkling that we might lose people during the transition and in fact we did lose the CEO, the COO, the CIO and a couple of key fund managers in a day. Which was obviously not the most perfectly structured deal.

You can be a fantastic fixed income fund manager for your whole career but by that stage I was ready for something different. It was a time when the bond market was fixated on non-farm payrolls and I thought – if I have to spend another Friday working up the whole month around this number … It became so tedious.

Mellon did offer me the CIO role but it didn't go smoothly. They wanted to put in their own CEO who already had another job as well. Overnight I met up with my colleagues and in the morning one of them said they didn't want me to be the CIO. This was disappointing because I thought I had a mandate. And then I realised I would probably have to leave the firm.

I decided to ask people to meet me and tell me why they didn't see me in that role, so at least I would know. It was a painful couple of hours, I have to admit, because when people talk in front of you, it's harder than being talked about behind your back. But the main issue was that they wanted someone with equity experience and also, perhaps, that I hadn't been there that long.

Then suddenly one person, who wasn't necessarily my greatest fan, said: "It was quite courageous of Helena to invite us all here. Maybe we should ask that she be the CEO?" Which was not exactly the turn in the conversation I was expecting.

Like a rabbit in the headlights, I said "I suppose so" and that was how it came about. It taught me a few things. You do have to take criticism and listen, and I think we all struggle with that. I certainly still struggle when people criticise me. I sometimes get criticised and I know they're wrong because they haven't understood where I'm coming from. But sometimes there's also very valid criticism that you can't just lump into that category.

I did make mistakes. Hopefully though, I learnt from them. It was a baptism of fire, I suppose.

I carried on running money for about three years but of course I became less and less good at that. It demands a full-time focus. But it is helpful that I have an investment background.

I feel it's something that keeps me very close to the key investors – more so than if I was from a business background. But obviously I had to learn the business side of it. So there's more than one way to be the CEO.

The Thirty Per Cent Club

The Thirty Per Cent Club is a group of chairs and chief executives taking action to create a better balance of men and women at all levels of their organisations as a business imperative rather than a "women's issue".

The club launched in the UK in 2010 with a goal of getting the company boards of all FTSE 100 firms to be 30% female by the end of 2015.

The idea has since been picked up internationally with other Thirty Per Cent Clubs now in place in countries such as the US, Australia, South Africa, Hong Kong and Malaysia.

As at the end of June 2015, 46 FTSE 100 companies had at least 25% women on their boards.

The 30% figure was chosen by Morrissey because research suggests this is the proportion when critical mass for a minority group is reached. At this stage, in a group setting, the voices of the minority become heard in their own right, rather than simply representing the minority.

She explains: "This resonated with what I'd been reading about group behaviour: if you're the only woman, you heard as a woman, or if you're the only man, you heard as a man. But, if you're one of three out of ten, you're heard more as a person."

She became aware that she might be in a position to make change when, as chief executive of Newton, younger women began asking her advice.

"I felt I had a responsibility to help the next generation," she says. "Perhaps it didn't always have to be a struggle and perhaps I could ease the path."

Morrissey's first attempt was to initiate a women's network within BNY Mellon. She invited speakers who would appeal to men as well as women, such as Karen Brady and Anna Ford. But while the events were popular, actual results were scant.

Disillusioned, Morrissey attended a lunch hosted by Goldman Sachs as part of its diversity week. She discovered that, despite their best intentions, other firms appeared to be stuck in the bracket of 10% to 15% of women at higher levels. She says, "Afterwards I thought we must all be doing something wrong because we have been doing this for decades and still not getting anywhere."

Eventually Morrissey hit on the idea of the Thirty Per Cent Club and that it should focus on company boards, which would be both measurable in terms of its aims and also symbolic of the contribution of women to a traditionally male environment.

Integral to the Club's success, however, has been the input from senior male executives.

Morrissey says, "Now I realise that if you have those on the inside in power helping those on the outside, then it goes a long way further than just women talking amongst ourselves."

Morrissey herself remains against quotas, considering them demeaning, and prefers business-led change to regulatory demands. She gives the example of Norway where women executives were drafted in to fill non-executive quotas on boards. The wholescale shift left the senior executive pipeline dry.

The Club's work now has a greater focus on supporting that pipeline. But boards remain a concern, especially in terms of refreshment.

Morrissey says, "There's about 10% of FTSE non-exec directors who have served on their boards for more than nine years. They're supposed to serve up to two terms, a third possibly, and then step down. So there is still a bit of self-feeding going on. But I do think a lot of attitudes are changing."

For Morrissey, the greatest achievement is that companies are more aware of the need for diversity. "The chairmen wouldn't have expressed it like this – it sounds too New Agey – but they get it that they didn't have the right balance of masculine and feminine energies. And that's quite a big breakthrough."

JW: You spend a great deal of time promoting women in business. Why is female participation so important?

HM: Differences of perspective are really valuable. It's a given now, that if you have homogenous boards, they don't challenge each other and so on.

It's not just stereotyping. Neuroscience suggests that women are more empathetic in terms of their natural hardwiring. Boys' brains are thought to be more systematic, while women are more consensus-building. Women produce a tenth of the male level of testosterone and so on.

These are big differences but they make us stronger together. I think we complement each other. The differences are to be celebrated. That's exciting for women coming through now. Whenever I speak to girls' schools or university students, I say not only that this is the moment for women in the workplace, but also that you can be yourself. You can be different.

I had to compromise. It might seem unlikely now but I did have to fit in enough to get that voice and that seat at the table. Now the men and women at the top get it and the new generation gets it. There is a bit more resistance in the middle.

But the realisation is that the balance is how we're supposed to be.

JW: What holds women back?

HM: There are several factors. Here in the UK, the cost and availability of childcare stands out a mile from everywhere else. We did a study a couple of years ago looking at all the OECD countries and on most criteria, the UK was fine, except for the cost of childcare. Here, it's a quarter of disposable income and the next worst country was something like 8%.

We did this other project recently when we asked women, particularly in the age group of 28 to 40, to talk about their experiences at work. The overwhelming response was that although the women said their partners were supportive, and that they themselves wanted to progress, they didn't feel supported in the workplace.

Two-thirds of the mothers in the survey said they worked flexibly but that they felt resented by their colleagues for doing so and they thought it was a career impediment. Conveniently, those who didn't work flexibly said they did resent their flexible working colleagues. So there was no argument about that point.

But if you're bright and you make a great contribution, does it matter that you don't sit at the same desk all the time?

My husband worked as a freelance journalist after we decided that one of us needed to be more at home. He was the natural choice but he also wanted to do it. He felt very intellectually fulfilled by what he was doing, but he wasn't going to develop his career in the same way as when he was doing long hours behind a Bloomberg news desk. So we've got to think more creatively, not just for women, but for companies.

JW: You think companies could be more flexible in their expectations?

HM: Definitely. The logical conclusion of this focus on women is that working men would have wider societal expectations about what makes a worthy life. So men could play more of a role, or have the opportunity to play more of a role, if they agree as a family how to bring up the children. It should be a little bit more fluid than the assumption that it's more the woman's job. We're a long way off that state but I do think we could be at the start of the process. The focus is off women on boards and much more on how to make more workplaces relevant for today.

JW: You're a chief executive with nine children. Do you think, as a female role model, you've set the bar too high?

HM: Some people do say it must be very off-putting for others. But then pulling your hair out and looking frazzled all the time doesn't necessarily work either.

Everybody's life is completely different. I didn't plan to have nine children, I planned to have five. Obviously there was a bit of a mistake along the way but a good one. And I didn't deliberately set out to become CEO at Newton, while the Thirty Per Cent Club was more born out of frustration rather than an attempt to change the world.

It is enormous though, the whole show. I have learned to sit down and think through all the different components of it and then to take one step at a time. And when I get fazed and overwhelmed, it's because I've failed to do that.

I always say as well – don't put people on a pedestal. Each of my days is full of triumphs and disasters, the same as it was when I was 21 and just starting out. In some ways, the scale of both the good and the bad things is more intense and bigger, but it's still the same dealing with them. I do get tired and I do have off moments, or days or weeks. I'm just human.

JW: You've said that you thought you were passed over for promotion at Schroder because you were pregnant. You also went to a comprehensive school. How did you cope with working in what has been quite a male, public school environment?

HM: I'm not really that fussed about not being inside a group. I never felt defined by being part of the group, and I realise that's been quite helpful. But not something you choose to be like, you just are.

Lots of things have happened along the way and sometimes it's hard not to mind. Sometimes people say things or make assumptions, even now, which show they think of me as a certain type of person because I'm a woman and I didn't go to the same school as they did. It's surprising that they do because I've been so public about the equality point of view.

I have learnt certain lessons. There was one meeting recently where I was the only woman in a big room of people. Someone said something incredibly patronising to me in a way that made me see red. So I swore at him, in front of all the people.

It was quite an eye-opener because he behaved differently towards me after that. I must emphasise that most of the men there were very supportive and everyone was slightly horrified by the way the conversation was going. I'm a big one for trying to get people on my side and working with people in a non-confrontational way but it doesn't always work. Sometimes you have to give as good as you get.

So I'm learning all the time. My generation has definitely had to adapt. For many years, I have felt like I can be myself at work but occasionally I do wonder whether, if I was a man and much more in the mainstream group, I would be less sensitive. But then I've seen young women, who expect the world to be equal, get very disappointed.

I too was very disappointed when I got passed over for promotion because there wasn't a good explanation for it, apart from the fact that I'd had a baby and there was some doubt over my commitment. You have to remember though that it's not personal usually. When someone says something very dispiriting, it's easy to feel they're talking about you when actually it's just their attitude in general. You have to try not to take it personally.

JW: What was the best thing about being a fund manager?

HM: The results-based work. It's great to have intellectual stimulation from your colleagues, but you probably get that in other professions as well. You can have great relationships with clients and of course every day in the market is different from the last. But the really great thing, not just for women but for anybody who wants to have other things going on in their life, is that no-one can quibble with you if you've delivered.

I don't think I could've done some of what I have done if I'd been, say, a corporate finance lawyer and transaction-based. Not with the children and so on. Unequivocally, I think it's a great career. It's very depressing that there are so few female fund managers and that's something I would like to help correct.

Do women make better fund managers than men?

Research published by Brad Barber and Terrance Odean in the *Quarterly Journal of Economics* in 2001 studied the effects of trading frequency and overconfidence in the investment world.

In a survey of 35,000 investors, the researchers found that women were less likely to make losses as a result of overtrading and overconfidence. However, they also found that women traded 68% less than men – which had a beneficial impact on transaction costs and the final return to investors.

Commenting on the research, Helena Morrissey says that she believes women tend to be more risk-aware and conscientious about reading material while paying less attention to hunches.

Another important female attribute is to "tend and befriend" when events turn sour, whereas men are more likely to "fight or flight" and sometimes find it difficult to accept they have made the wrong decision.

"Every active fund manager makes bad calls," Morrissey says. "You can get completely hunkered down and that's not necessarily the right approach, because you end up in a hole digging yourself in."

Aware that these distinctions are massively generalised, Morrissey says that a balance of approaches is the best solution.

"One way is not better or worse than the other. You have to have huge conviction to be a successful active fund manager. I've seen women struggle to make that big call and also men go it alone and not get the result. None of us have the monopoly on great ideas and you need sounding boards. And that's sometimes where women can be quite proficient – in bringing people into their decisions."

JW: What's your understanding of risk?

HM: Now I'm conscious of what I said about women generally, but I think I'm a risk-taker. I wouldn't have taken the CEO role if I had been analysing the pros and cons of the situation. I suppose I put my head above the parapet on certain uncomfortable issues. But I'm not cavalier about risk. I'm very risk conscious about some of the basics in running the business on the regulatory front and also the risks to the industry if we don't get on the front foot on certain aspects that are now being challenged.

JW: Like what?

HM: Fees. Transparency of fees and commission. The whole litany of things around cost. And the value added from active management.

JW: Are there any parallels between your investment life and your personal life?

HM: The key to investing is knowing when you're wrong and doing something about it. I had a terrible year in 1999 when I was long and wrong and it was just awful. I had a child that year too and physically I had problems afterwards because she had been premature. The whole year was pretty much a disaster.

It's a life lesson really. You can be rock bottom but you've got to find the strength of character and help from around you to go back and pick it up. Again, I couldn't do that on my own without people who supported and encouraged me so I didn't feel so isolated.

Having a large family also teaches you to be quite objective about different skills. I think I've become better at understanding people through having my family.

Chapter 13

The Outsider at the Heart of Change

Saker Nussebeih interviewed by Lawrence Gosling

Having entered the City by 'fluke' in 1987, Saker Nussebeih, a Palestinian by birth, joined one of the great 'outsider' firms in the City's modern history, Mercury Asset Management (MAM). He joined Hermes in 2009 as head of investment and assumed the chief executive role in 2012. He says that really outstanding fund managers "always occupy the extremes of the spectrum of confidence and lacking in confidence at the same time".

Lawrence Gosling: How did you get into being a fund manager?

Saker Nussebeih: In the summer of 1986, I was writing up my doctorate in medieval history, my wife was writing up hers in politics. I was looking for a job and Mrs. Thatcher had killed funding to the universities. There was an offer in *The Times* for a junior research fellowship in £6,000. On the same page, there was an advertisement for a PA for somebody in the City for £18,000 and I was handsome and young and vain, and I thought I look pretty, I can type and answer a phone and

£18,000 is a hell of a lot of money. So I came to the City entirely by mistake. I had no idea what shares were. The only economics I'd done was at A-level.

By a fluke, I ended up at Mercury Asset Management (MAM). Mercury in the mid-80s had a lot of cheap graduates and they used them as slave labour and then expected them to leave. I remember buying the equivalent of *The City for Dummies*. That was an amazing introduction because I came with no preconceptions; I turned up and I asked some really stupid questions like "why is this stock cheaper on a P/E of eight against this stock with a P/E of 10?" I asked all the questions that they took for granted.

LG: Does that inquisitiveness come from being interested in history?

SN: I think so. I didn't realise it at the time, but actually I was laying the foundation for asking all the things I ask now, and the history allowed me to look at the big picture. It's like all these things in life, luck plays a huge part ultimately. I was lucky I was at Mercury because it taught you real fundamental analysis and they worked you really hard. A graduate trainee was the guy who got the sandwiches, and did the binding for the presentations for the clients, and did the research in his spare time, and wrote the minutes for meetings, and did odd jobs, and learnt on the job. Some of the greatest fund managers this country has produced worked there.

Everybody knows the names of Stephen Zimmerman, Leonard Licht and Carol Galley; fewer know somebody like

James D'Albaic who I think was one of the greats and I had the privilege of sitting next to him. He taught me the secret of fund management. After two years of sitting next to him he said to me "Well, Saker, I suppose I've got to teach you about fund management, haven't I?" And I said "Yes, that would be very kind, sir." He said "Well, there's one rule of fund management; if it looks too good to be true, it is." And do you know what? It's absolutely right.

LG: There must have been other lessons?

SN: From James here is the lesson: during the crash of 1987, he did two things. One is he understood markets are truly cyclical. His reference point was the crash of '72-'73. That gave perspective. While everyone was panicking, he wasn't. The second thing he did which was really interesting, which I think people should do more now, is he switched off the screen and said, "Carry on with your work researching companies. This is irrelevant." The way we talk about markets now reminds me of the races. So if you switch on the TV stations and look at the markets, or indeed read the newspapers, it's like listening to commentary on the races. This is not investment, this is trading. And so what he taught me was that investment was very long-term.

Carol taught me in many ways about management. But what she was really good at was finding young people who were really good at analysing companies and doing fundamental research, and then empowering them to take very large stakes. Leonard taught me about engaging with the company that you own; it's not just owning the companies, you've got to sit and talk to the boards. It doesn't mean you just sit and listen to what they're saying to you, but you actually engage with them about their business. And ultimately Zimmerman taught me about the passion. He was the first person I knew who would call from holidays, which was unheard of at the time, to talk about his portfolio. It is this obsession that makes really good fund managers.

LG: How do you differentiate between passion and people who are just paranoid about their portfolio?

SN: Portfolio managers, as opposed to traders, take positions in companies which generally are very, very long-term. I once used to go around saying the only difference between truly outstanding fund managers and mediocre fund managers is that the really outstanding ones remember five-and-a-half out of every 10 mistakes they make; the mediocre ones only remember five. It's about remembering.

I've thought long and hard about what makes a fund manager. And I've come to a conclusion that good fund managers – I'm going to offend all my friends and colleagues and potential clients now – are essentially psychologically flawed people.

Your first test of whether they are a good manager or not is to find out if they're psychologically flawed. It doesn't mean they're good if they're flawed, but flawed is a precursor to them being good. Because most people will wake up in the morning and they will either feel confident or lacking in confidence, depending on whether they slept well, whether the dog woke them up in the morning, whether they had a good breakfast. And then they'll change during the day; that's just normal human nature.

Really outstanding fund managers always occupy the extremes of the spectrum of confidence and lacking in confidence at the same time. This is not normal. They're always obsessed that they might be wrong, but they actually believe they're right. Now that is different from being obsessed with ticks in the market. It's not the same thing. That's obsession about the idea, not about the ticks. Really, really great fund managers like Buffett; when he was asked what is your ideal holding time for a company, he looked at the journalist and said "forever". He just couldn't understand the question.

It means a tick in the price is an irrelevance. And I've come across people like that. Does that mean that then you're not a full human being outside? No it doesn't. You've got to compartmentalise. I think where people get it wrong is they obsess too much with it and it becomes overpowering. Then they forget why they're doing it. It's great to have the skill but the skill is simply a means to an end. You've got to think about what's the purpose of this? And not a lot of people ask that. When I joined, we used to say we help people retire, we look after people's retirement funds. That's a very holistic answer actually. Nowadays you ask somebody what they do for a living and they say, "Oh, I run small cap US." Really?

LG: Looking after somebody else's money is a great honour?

SN: It is. The vast majority of money we run is money for ordinary people, through their pension schemes. They're going to retire, in the vast majority of cases, with an annual income that is less on average than our monthly income as an industry. Now what we do, if we do it right, they get a bit more that might help them, depending where they are in the world, afford a better holiday, afford more heating in the winter, afford a better wheelchair.

When I went through the ranks (at MAM) I started going out to the States and we ran some money for a very small state fund. I remember at one stage going out on my own and making a presentation and the script said that we'd done a really good job because the portfolio had outperformed the benchmark. We were negative but less than the benchmark. It was one of these small towns in the States where we turn up and the participants come and listen. They sat there and I got up and I'm meant to say what a great job I've done. And I looked at them and these were retired teachers and I remember saying to them, sorry, I lost money. Which is not the correct thing to say if you're trying to sell yourself as being great fund managers.

LG: So where do you think you got that humility from because Mercury had a reputation for being an arrogant firm?

SN: I think Mercury was. I think Mercury was both arrogant and for a reason; it was the outsider. It was a firm of outsiders that had made it in the City. And they were very good at what they did. But that meant that they developed a culture that was quite hard and in some ways it was the ultimate in Darwinism. They therefore had a very strong reputation of being arrogant. But we were arrogant because when we looked at a sector, we did our own research, we knew as much as the broking analysts, if not more. Quite often a lot more. There was an arrogance because the performance was very strong. There was an arrogance because the internal selection was so vicious that if you survived it, you were one of the elite. Why was I different? I think I was lucky because I wasn't from that milieu to start off with. I'm the ultimate outsider in some ways.

LG: They were a group of outsiders?

SN: Yes, it's interesting. Some of Zimmerman's family died in the Holocaust. Carol Galley grew up in Blackpool. She was Jewish, a woman, in the City. She hated cigars, because it was old-fashioned. The others were a bunch of outcast Etonians. They weren't Etonians who had made it, they were Etonians that nobody else wanted. Outcast Etonians and outcast Jews coming together to create something amazing.

Now why was I different? When I came to England, I came to study. I'm an Arab, a Palestinian. I was born and raised in Jerusalem so I went through a war and all that rubbish and I came here as a student and I fell in love with England. And it wasn't a financial falling in love with England, I fell in love with the idea of England and what the English stand for. I'm not saying British, I'm being very specific. This is England.

In that sense I'm a very odd immigrant. It's the whole thing about why is it the English have an inherent bolshiness, and because of this inherent bolshiness, actually, liberty was born in England. Then you look at second generation immigrants, the Bangladeshi community, and look at the children. They're Brits, even in the bolshiness of their fanatical Islam, they're Brits. It's bizarre. They did a survey among Muslims in Britain versus Muslims in Europe and on every single metric, they feel more integrated, happier. And then are they happy with their life? And the answer is no. Of course not, what Brit says to you "I'm happy"?

I have always felt that any position I have financially is a remarkable privilege and that therefore I owe the society that I live in something in return. That meant I was always perhaps more conscious than my colleagues that ultimately I am a servant of the people whose money I run.

LG: Have you developed your own form of what engagement means, to include the more socially responsible elements?

SN: Yes. The engagement that I was always interested in was much more longer-term. I could see how short-term gain could destroy long-term gain. There was a company I used to love called Rentokil that had a very simple business model, based on the fact that you can never, never kill mice. You can't – if you have mice in your house, tough, they'll never go away. It was a repeat business. It's when they tried to do other things, and they did other acquisitions and went into services and scaffolding, it looked great for two or three years but actually they destroyed their business model.

The conversation you have with a company is about sustainability. Ultimately that's what we're talking about. The sector that I ended up looking after (at MAM) was the insurance sector. What struck me about the insurance sector was that Lloyds of London had survived 200 years of wars, of revolutions, of major disasters, or economic downturns perfectly adequately but was brought down by asbestos. Asbestos is an environmental problem.

What was it about England that was so great? It's the checks and balances. And that applies to everything in life. Badly governed companies have no checks and balances so you might have a genius as CEO, but you still need checks and balances. That's where the governance comes in.

LG: There are a lot of fund management companies around where individuals are earning a very good living for producing not-a-fantastic-return for a lot of people?

SN: Absolutely. There's a conundrum at the heart of the fund management industry. I hate the word alpha. Let's talk about skill. Skill is real. And yet there's a massive industry that's almost entirely based on the idea that you can create skill in a factory. Fund management companies have been trying to do this for many, many years. They talk about processes, they talk about teams, they talk about structures, philosophies and so on, but the reality is that for many, many years, active management has been effectively a version of just a little bit of beta, not even turbo-charged beta.

You're right, you can't tell the difference between a good fund manager and a bad fund manager if you have a short time period. So you have two problems; the first one is to really tell statistically if somebody is good or not, they've got to be a fund manager for a long time.

The second element is that the skill is actually beating the index consistently and over a long period, and it's more than just process. Particularly in the '90s and the noughties, the phrase that was being used was we design product. It's like cars. We're selling product. The factories, particularly the French were very fond of this, the manufacturing of fund management. Well, it ain't like that. Fund management is in essence an artisan job. I'm fond of calling our teams "artisans" because artisanship is somewhere that's at the periphery of a process which is manufacturing but also art. And it's partly learnt, and partly innate. That's fund management.

In the noughties you had the beta jockeys. The hedge fund industry grew on the back of levering. Now levering simply multiplies your returns. If your result's going to be 3% and you lever 10 times, lo and behold it becomes 30%. In a rising market, it looked like they were geniuses and they weren't really. They were just simply levered players. It was the worst case of lack of skill.

The acid test is if you strip all that out, how do you recognise a good fund manager? It's a matter of just looking at their long-term track record, ultimately, and you have to understand the context and whether they're really adding value through skill as opposed to something else. Skill can be a variety of things. Skill can be fundamental analysis, skill can be the ability to understand long-term trends. Which is a different kind of skill but perfectly valid.

I argue that most people don't do fundamental research. Going and talking to a company and a company seminar is not research. Talking to the chief executive of a company is not research. Research is a lot more boring. I think the noughties glamorised fund management. Fund management is not a glamorous business. Fund management is a very boring business. It's simply looking at things, item for item, trying to understand them, trying to understand the business models and seeing the companies, trying to make judgements on them, based on the long term. It's just tedious. And then having the knack of working out that something is going to work or not. And to be able to recognise mistakes and turn them round.

LG: In the last 25 years PEPs and ISAs have opened up the world of fund management but arguably less certainty about the outcome?

SN: You're right; it makes it harder to get at what fund management is. Part of what we're trying to do as an industry is pretend that we're very sophisticated. This started in the noughties with the hedge funds. We use really sophisticated terms. We believe that computer powers have enhanced our ability to become better financial whizz-kids. The new generation of fund managers studied finance. They've all

189

heard of Markowitz and modern financial theory and Sharpe and so on, and so they think this is a science. And it isn't, economics is not a science. It's not physics; there are no laws of economics. Not a single law of economics is either observable or repeatable; it's just conjecture.

But it gives the feeling that you're dealing with science and that gives you a false confidence. That's important because I think part of the skill of fund management is working out that you're wrong. To do that, you must not take what you're doing too seriously. I know it sounds bizarre but you must accept that you can be wrong.

So I'm the man, God help me, who flew out to Finland in 1992 because that was my country to interview a company called Nokia that used to make televisions and mobile phones as a small business, and had stopped making rubber. I'm the man who said to them – because I was from Mercury and I knew things and I had read management books – "you should concentrate on your point of excellence which is making televisions because the Japanese will completely annihilate you". But at least I knew that I knew nothing about fund management and I went back to England and I asked some friends of mine at university about how mobile phones work and they mentioned the word software to me, which I had never heard of before in my life, and they explained what software was and the difference between software and hardware. And I flew back six months later and I'm eating my words. But it's that ability. I knew it wasn't a science.

LG: I'm always mistrustful when I hear fund managers say the market's wrong?

SN: The market's neither right nor wrong. The market is the market – it's simply a weighing machine. So you're right, the market's neither right nor wrong. Fund managers need to be arrogant enough to believe in what they're doing but we go back to this thing about the psychological flaw. They need to be arrogant enough to believe in what they're doing but they also need to be humble enough to always think that they might be wrong. That is the way to find good fund managers. It's that they can be both at the same time.

The thing about showmen is important because I suffered from the opposite. Because essentially, I was trained to be a lecturer, I talked well. But that meant that in the first part of my career when the City was full of fund managers who did not speak well, there was an assumption that I can't be good technically. That was the bias of the time. It's changed now but in the early '80s it took a long time to convince colleagues at MAM that technically I'm okay, but I can actually enunciate what I want to say.

But we've gone the other way now. So I have an outstanding fund manager who is an appalling presenter. But fund management in some ways is the easiest thing to judge. Numbers talk. It's as simple as that. And the numbers, and this is where it's important, are not simply the absolute numbers. It's the risk-adjusted numbers. It's how much return for how much risk. Of all the jargon that people have to learn, Sharpe ratios, information ratios, are the most important. And both over the long-term are the most important, not the short-term.

If somebody has performed consistently over the long term, he or she is good, simple as that. Then worry about how they do it and you will find that these people combine arrogance with humility and you will find that they'll change their mind when it's right, but it's an art to know when not to change your mind also. There are times when you don't let the market bully you, if you like, and you will find that they will have periods which underperform. There's only one fund manager I know of who had a very long streak of outperformance, a guy called Glen Bickerstaff (at Trust Company of the West) who has retired now, in the States. He had almost a Warren Buffett-type of portfolio; only ever had 25 stocks.

LG: Talk to me about the tyranny of benchmarks.

SN: I'll tell you a story. When I first came to Hermes, I had the privilege of meeting someone who used to be on the Barings pension scheme. He described to me the history of the Barings pension scheme. Barings Bank was very old and very successful. For a long, long time, the pension scheme was run by a bunch of old codgers who sat together in a room; I think it was called the Widows and Orphans Fund. They sat in the room and talked about things. There were times when they thought that putting money somewhere safe was worthwhile, and they just kept the money in the bank. There were times when they had lots of stocks and there were times when they had very few stocks. And they employed that most precious of commodities, common sense, and they knew that the point of it was to make money.

Then sometime in the 1960s, benchmarks came in and the point stopped being about making money. Fund managers, because their livelihood both in terms of how they're remunerated and in terms of what they sell, became linked to benchmarks. The benchmarks became the be all and end all.

Then think about what the benchmark means. The benchmark is a collection of stocks where the most expensive stocks became a bigger component of the benchmark. We saw in the run-up to 2000 what that meant with Vodafone in the UK. And the debt benchmark is even crazier. Then you have this idea of "I can't find the skill, therefore I'll buy the benchmark". Then the derivative of that is "I'll buy the derivative on the benchmark because actually I'm not investing at all, I'm just playing market factors". Then you get the even crazier idea of "it doesn't matter what the companies do, so I don't have any contact with the companies, I'm just buying the factor of exposure of the company". Sorry, this is not investment.

Investment at its heart is very simple. It's about making money. Go back to basics. Sometime in the 19th century, there were agents who worked typically for very rich people, they'd go down to Plymouth and they'd see which ships were coming in and what company they belonged to. They'd observe which tavern was being frequented by the seamen and they'd go to the ship owner and say we'd like to become partners in your venture. And they'd go to the tavern owner and say to them we'd like to become your partner. That's fund management. You just find out the right business and you make money.

Benchmarks are a way for others who try to work out skill, but they miss the point. People who have skill, generally speaking, pay less attention to benchmarks. Because they understand the point is to make money.

Apparently the new thing now that all the markets are excited about are absolute return funds. This is a new invention, wow! Really? We're laughing but it's not funny. There is this disease that's entered the fund management business and this disease is this belief that there's a science called financial science. That if you understand the mathematics and you put in the formulas, then you win. Sorry, that's not investment. And by the way, it's all based on unprovable fact. Somehow we've lost sight of the idea that what we do is we make educated guesses to become partners – and this is important – to try to make a return which is a real return.

Go back to the 19th century when the Rothschilds dealt in government stocks, they understood what that meant. It was an investment in the government. Now we have risk-free rates. What is a risk-free rate? There's no such thing. It's nonsense. So we've got to come back as fund managers to understanding what we're about is trying to take the money that's been entrusted to us, by small investors on average, and actually think about how we can enhance that return for them over the long term.

LG: Do you think environmental issues can be part of a long-term sustainable investment thesis, or is it just something that people with conscience have an interest in?

SN: I think it started off as a fad. Essentially there are some hippies out there who want to buy some stocks. I think there's a move now among CEOs who think that this is the future so let's talk about integrating it. But the truth is that if you're not integrating environmental concern in any kind of investment then you're not looking at the risks of that investment. The environment permeates everything we do because we're changing the world that we live in. I'm not proselytising. I'm just describing fact. We are changing the world that we live in and we are changing it in a particular way. Environment does make a difference.

Those of us old enough will remember the Bhopal disaster in India. That's an environmental disaster, ultimately. If a company relies on essentially indentured labour in emerging markets, it's not a very secure source of supply and that might disrupt it. If a company is making too much profit in this country, without passing on some of its wages to the labour force, that means that the entire structure is not safe because at some stage there is going to be a backlash which is going to limit the freedom of the free market economy because people are not going to stand for it.

I was listening to the wireless and David Cameron was telling companies they should give more of their profits to workers. Cameron, right? The Etonian upper class chappie whose father was a stockbroker, telling companies you've got to give some to these poor chaps at the bottom otherwise – why? Because it's not sustainable. Now he's not a hippie.

These are ideas that should be integrated and that's what we do here in Hermes. We integrate them because you have to have sustainability. You have to preserve the eco-system, the financial eco-system and the problem with what happened in the run-up to 2008 is that because there were no checks and balances, the eco-system was essentially fractured.

And by the way, the eco-system is not healed. All that's happened is the mistakes that were made by investment banks and some insurance companies based on their assumption there's a science to financial dealing – and ultimately greed and a lack of understanding of risk – has resulted in a massive amount of debt on the world economy, which the banks no longer hold on their books, but you and me (and our sons and daughters) and will hold for a generation. That's not solved. That's simply shunting it around.

We've got to try and find a way in which this is not repeated. One way is to try to make sure this is not repeated is by looking at all the risk that is inherent in investment. Is the business model we're investing in sustainable?

This then goes back into sustainability which is the story of Rentokil. I want my profit for 20 years, I don't want my profit for one year. Common sense will say to you sustainability is important. Environment is important. Governance is important. These are risks that should be taken into every single decision; it's mainstream, not periphery.

LG: Does that mean that there is a natural sustainable level of profit and as an investor you should be happy with that?

SN: Yes, I'm not going to blame the Americans, but why this thing of you have to be more? There is a level. There's a cycle in life and there is a natural level to which it is good for a business to grow that level and collectively, the global economy, we're growing at the level anyway. You've got to be careful and you've got to look at sustainability of the business model long-term. You've got to look at other environmental concerns that come in and other checks and balances. If you're not doing that in any investment whatever you call yourself, I think you're not looking at all the risk.

LG: What does a good fund management company look like from the outside to a private investor?

SN: Number one, they don't use complicated language to describe anything. It's a basic rule. If they can't tell you what it is that they do in the simplest of language, there's something really wrong because they're obfuscating. Secondly the language is about you and not about them. A lot of fund management companies talk about themselves: "We are the best managers, we have these qualities, we're really good". Excuse me; you work for me.

And the third one is that the people that they employ actually are people with long-term track records and you can see that they've had good years and bad years and they don't hide this. Are they the sort of company that want you to be there for the long-term? Are they the sort of company who say this is a business that we're not skilled at, rather than say "Yes, we can do everything"? A bit of humility. It's common sense. If you speak to people who are in the business, the fund managers themselves, then they talk with common sense. It's the most underrated of British qualities.

Chapter 14

There Must be More Than This

Stewart Cowley interviewed by Lawrence Gosling

Stewart Cowley was until the summer of 2015 fixed income director for Old Mutual Global Investors and ran the Global Strategic Bond. He has embarked upon a new venture, Northfield Strategic Investors. Before joining Old Mutual, Cowley was head of fixed income at Newton Investment Management from 2000 to 2009.

In this wide-ranging interview he describes how a boy who grew up on a council estate in the North East managed to reach the top of the fund management industry, and that he says his job is to create a decent return for ordinary investors as crucial to his outlook. "If you expect to literally drain every pound or dollar out of the markets every single day of your career, it will drive you mad," he says.

Lawrence Gosling: Your route into fund management was not typical?

Stewart Cowley: I worked in a steel works, which was really weird. I'm not who you think I am; I come from a council estate in the North East of England. This was never supposed to happen to me. When I was a kid, I had one phrase that went round and round in my head. I don't know where it came from but it was "there must be more than this". I had it from about the age of eight.

I got my O-levels and everything – and I did all kinds of things, played in orchestras and stuff like that; nobody had ever played a musical instrument in my family before, it was all very, very strange. Then my parents said, "You're going to work," at the age of 16. I said "Okay," so I got an apprenticeship at British Steel. I left school in June, turned up in the September, they gave me a hard hat, overalls and some great big hobnail boots, and said, "You are now an apprentice," in this Dante's hell of a place, where people died on a regular basis. I looked at this right at the beginning and I thought, "This is just not me at all". Fortunately they sent us to night school and we had day release as well, so that's where I got my A-levels. I worked my socks off for two years and I got my qualifications and a sponsorship from British Steel to go to University.

LG: How did your parents react?

SC: They simply couldn't understand it at all. First-generation University, you're making it up as you go along. Every single day you're reinventing yourself. I knew I was clever; I didn't have a focus yet. When I did my first degree, it was just a relief not being in a steel works, so every day was a joyous day. I realised that this was really quite a smart thing to do, not to go back to a steel works, so I thought, "Why not go a step further and go and do a doctorate?" Which again was just ridiculous, I never thought I'd do that kind of thing, that was for other people. And I went to my tutor and said, "Look, I've got this research idea," and he said "Well, you can't do it here at Manchester; you've got to go to Oxford or Cambridge". I got an interview eventually, from Oxford. I was very lucky. In the end I spent five years at Oxford.

The thing is it was all about the motivation: there must be more than this. The excitement of being a scientist and the idea of doing something which nobody had ever done before, or thinking something or seeing something that nobody had ever done before was just thrilling. It was utterly thrilling.

LG: What led you into a "proper" career?

SC: That's the accidental fund manager thing. I played the double bass in a jazz quartet, and the drummer was an economist and I said I was thinking about getting married. I was getting paid £6,000 a year as a Fellow at Oxford University and bear in mind the secretaries probably got paid about £12,000. We were very, very drunk indeed and he (the drummer) said what about the bank thing? If you want to earn a lot of money, go and be a banker. So I said I'm going to do that. The next day I went down to the Oxford careers place and got a handful of forms for banks, filled them all in and got all these interviews. I turned up at the first interview, for Donaldson Lufkin & Jenrette (DLJ) a week early. They turned me away at reception and said come back next week. I went back a week later.

It's 1987 by this point, they were plundering Oxford and Cambridge for anyone who's numerate, who can think, who can put a sentence together. I got this letter through the door one Saturday morning and I opened it and it was this £20,000 offer from DLJ to go over (to New York) for a three-month training period, the wife can come too. We got married on the basis of this.

So you talk about motivation. It was just this kind of thing – how far can you take it? If you're reinventing yourself every single day, you've no expectations of history behind you; you wake up each day and say, "What am I going to do?"

LG: Presumably there were no expectations from anybody around you?

SC: Their preference was that I would go back to the North East and get a job at British Steel and that would be me for 35 years. They never had any regard for it. They didn't have very much regard for my academic career either. Interesting that when my mother died, they looked in her purse and they found a press cutting of me in a newspaper, which she carried around in her purse.

LG: If you had, you'd have been out work by the middle of the '80s?

SC: Absolutely right. In a parallel universe, there is another Stewart Cowley who didn't do the route that I took and is now sitting in the North East of England twiddling his thumbs until he dies. Thinking about what might have been.

LG: So you're in the markets …

SC: I was lost for about three years. I was really lost. I did not understand what was going on. I came from a scientific background so I was trained to have big thoughts, and then you go and test your assumptions. If it works then you try and work out why you could be wrong. That's how science works. It's not about reinforcement. It's about whether your theory survives your own interrogation.

But the market was weird. Because you go, "Why has the market done this today? Because of the inflation numbers." Next day you walk in and go, "Okay, inflation is doing this, yes, I know, but it's gone the other way. Why? Because of a different thing over here. So where is the logic in this pseudo-science which is building itself up around it?" Every time I saw something which I thought made sense, it just disappeared like tissue paper. I was lost, completely lost.

DLJ fired the graduate intake after the 1987 crash, and I found myself out of a job. I'd bought a house in Walthamstow, put £5,000 deposit down, and was out of work.

Eventually I turned up at this tiny little bond boutique, there were six of us working there, called Cheval Investments. It was dedicated to bond fund management and it had this new-fangled thing called the spreadsheet. I looked at this and thought, "Oh well, I'll have a go at this". This was 1988. I started working with it and nine months after coming out of university, I was put in charge of $1bn on a spreadsheet.

LG: Do you think you had more of a natural feel for it, because the process you were using was more scientific?

SC: The first thing I learnt was actually constructing things properly and mathematically gave you an advantage. The first thing was just really the appliance of science and technology to do really, really simple maths, and you could beat the market. Nine times out of 10 you would win. And so I kind of worked this out. It was very, very straightforward, it was O-Level maths, nothing fancy about it. I got taught a couple of lessons about clients at the time as well, about service and the end user.

Then the next thing was I got headhunted to go to John Govett after a few years. I was put in charge of a very controversial gilt fund, which was essentially burning capital to create an income, Very, very controversial. This is actually one of the things in my career which I'm really, really proud of which was that I worked out a bit of maths where you could do both things; you could preserve the capital and also deliver the income stream. I worked out how you did it.

I'm so proud of that because I got this phone call from this guy and he said to me, "My mother lives in a nursing home and can you just explain to me why the capital value of her investment is going down?" She uses this to pay for her nursing fees. I told him why and actually the great thing that happened is it went from the bottom of the fourth quartile to the top of the first quartile. It was at that point that I connected with real people. It was not just a game but there are real people at the end of this.

If you ever lose sight of that, you have lost it. That's why I have spent a career getting rid of people who think that they come to work each day in order to create the bonus for themselves using other people's money. If it goes right, they stick their hands out, and if it goes wrong they say see you next year. Another click of the wheel. So success is rewarded and failure is compensated. No thank you. Not interested. Because if they don't have that real connection, it means they don't understand what they're doing.

On a couple of occasions, people have said to me, "Why don't you go into politics?" I've said, "Look, I think I've done more good for society, in terms of if you add it up in my career, I've literally made hundreds of millions of dollars extra for ordinary people over and above what they could have expected from the markets in general, and I think that's probably done more good in society than sitting inside the House of Commons waving order papers."

LG: Do you feel slightly guilty because you get paid well for doing something you actually enjoy?

SC: I don't decide what I get paid. Society does. My brother-in-law works in A&E in Scotland, in Edinburgh. I can guarantee you right now that if you ever have an accident, the person that you want in charge of your life is my brother-in-law. I don't know how much he gets paid, but how can you possibly equate life with money? How can we put a greater value on money than we do on life in a sense? I don't decide that, society does.

We're judged every single day. It's almost too easy to judge us in some respects and that's why a whole industry has brewed up around us, commentary, analysis, individual motivation, back stories, that kind of thing. That's the other thing I also say to younger fund managers: "Try not to attach your self-esteem to a level of the market or where you are. It's very difficult, especially if you're very committed to it. But for your own sanity, do not attach yourself because it will take you up or down in a day, in a week, over the months, and it will get to you, it will seek you out."

LG: Are you conscious of a point in your career where you realised that actually you couldn't judge your own personal worth by what you achieved as a fund manager?

SC: That's quite interesting actually because for me it goes hand in hand with something else. If you go back to when I was at DLJ, fund management was regarded as pretty low down the scale. Then something happened in the late '80s; we went from being the exciting end of accountancy to having to be able to write, speak, structure an entertaining presentation, deliver it in a way which people were confident in you as an individual, go on the television, the radio. Suddenly you had to be this entirely different person, with mathematics, sociology, economics, politics, animal instinct. What's been asked of us increasingly is that you are a more and more rarefied person. What we're offering is not just a return, which obviously everybody is due and everybody is paying for, and that's your primary motivation. But also they're seeking certainty in an uncertain world. And that's what we sell.

LG: Do you think you're selling certainty by being more accessible?

SC: The thing is that as you get older, what I find is that you're not necessarily saying anything very different to what you were saying when you were, say, 30, but when you are 45, people start listening to you.

But to me a career in fund management is about self-doubt. It is constant worry and doubt. Not so much in terms of consequences for yourself, but this is a great intellectual puzzle that you're trying to work out. Because there are real people behind it. I say to young fund managers, "You're letting yourself in for a lifetime of worry. If you go back to your big house at the weekend and you walk in and you've got your lovely wife (or husband) and your lovely kitchen and you've got a nice car outside, it feels sort of okay but not terribly real. Because you know that it's Friday night and you've go and do it again on Monday morning."

LG: Where's the cut-off point so that worry doesn't tip over into a general mental health issue, for example?

SC: I've seen two or three very sad instances in the course of my career where people have been tipped over the edge by it. I think you have to learn how to put boundaries around it. It's about what is reasonable to expect of yourself. It's about understanding what is reasonable to expect of you and what you're capable of. If you expect to literally drain every pound or dollar out of the markets every single day of your career, it will drive you mad. That's why you've got to put some protecting boundary around yourself – and you can only get that by being through several cycles. Knowing what's reasonable. Knowing what you should you expect of yourself. No, you shouldn't have expected yourself to guess that the oil price was going to drop by 50% in the fourth quarter of 2014.

LG: So do you need to have made one or two painful mistakes and then learnt from those?

SC: Yes, it's the only way to learn. Unfortunately other people pay for it. All you can hope is you do as little damage or you can limit the damage as much as possible. This is where the introspection comes in. This is where the balance between the extrovert and the introvert comes from. The inner voice. That will lead you places where you wouldn't normally go to, left to your own devices. It will take you to extraordinary conclusions. And actually if you think about what we do for a living, it is often the extraordinary conclusion which actually makes a real difference.

There is a worry that comes with that inasmuch as we seem to have an industry based on catastrophic thinking because of it. People want to rush towards the extraordinary conclusion because they think, for whatever reason, either it will get them attention, or it will differentiate them from the crowd, but they don't quite understand that they may be deluding themselves into a catastrophic conclusion which isn't real. Now I've only done it three times, four times in my career, where I've come to extraordinary conclusions which have turned out to be absolutely right. I think about 1994, when I sold every derivative out of the company just before Nick Leeson blew up. I think about when I was at Newton and I wrote an article in the middle of 2007 saying – I've got it at home so I know it's true – the US housing market is falling to pieces.

I remember I was in my home office late one night and had the long bond on a Bloomberg screen, and it just kept on ticking up by another point. And at this point I was short; I was underweight the index. I remember just thinking about it and saying, "Right, there's something in the system here that we're not seeing, which will reveal itself one day. This is nothing to do with the economy, someone's going bust."

And so I went long. The Newton International Bond Fund which I was running at the time returned 45% over the year. And if I'm absolutely honest with you, I never expected that, the magnitude of it. But I just knew there was something wrong. You could see it, feel it, and you knew the numbers, that kind of thing. You make a couple of calls like that in your career and I think that makes you a good person.

But I think there's a great tendency these days for people to look for the extraordinary where it isn't there. What's really changed since 2007 is that we did brew up a pseudo-scientific investment and valuation approach to what we did, equities, fixed income, currencies. Models were everywhere, fair value was everywhere, the data set was there, you could analyse it for 20 or 30 years and it was like a Newtonian machine.

What has happened in the last seven years is that's been blown out of the water. Many valuations models do not work anymore. Decisions which affected the market were made behind closed doors by central bankers, which you could not analyse. You absolutely could not get what was going to happen next. The systematic approach – the macro vision of things – to try and get this right on a consistent basis was almost impossible.

If you go back to the stuff about boundaries and what's reasonable to expect of people. I think there is a big mismatch between what fund managers should and could expect of themselves, and the amount of money they're getting paid. The responsibility hasn't changed but the predictability of it has. And I wonder, deep inside myself, what is that saying about the system that we're working within? Because quantitative easing was blatant market manipulation. That was the purpose of it. The out-and-out purpose. How effective it was is another story. But we now work in a deeply manipulated system.

LG: Is the challenge for you then to figure out how that manipulation might unfold, or to get a clear handle on exactly which parts of the system are being manipulated?

SC: Well clearly the idea of the Americans has been to look after the financial systems and hope the economy responds to it. They looked after the stock market, they pumped up the bond market to a degree, everybody got all of their wealth back that they lost in the disastrous two-year period, plus another $15trillion that they shouldn't have had. So what you have is a pumped up financial system, and a moribund economy. They're not synonymous with each other anymore, as they used to be. Probably one of my mistakes in the last 18 months at Old Mutual was that I expected that when you took a corset off the system, that normal service would be resumed, and it didn't happen in the US. Something worse happened; bond yields fell. We are left in a high-reaction, highly-volatile system where it has very little linkage to fundamental economic data being pushed out daily that we used to rely upon to guide our decision making. It's gone.

LG: Do you think one of the issues is that the world is more data-driven but the data is a lot less reliable so it makes it harder?

SC: I think that's true. Take non-farm payrolls for example; we used to hang on its every word. Now? It comes out, and it can be a really great number and we expect economic expansion, bond yields to rise, the usual mechanistic view and it does completely the opposite. And you're sitting there thinking, okay, how does a fund manager with a responsibility to clients to structure a portfolio in a way that they can understand – which will behave in a predictable way given the macroeconomic scenario we're talking about – deliver what they expect? It's become increasingly difficult to do that, I have to say.

So I've modernised my thinking in that I take a long-short view of things. What I've done is move into a modern era of saying: "You know what? I don't know everything, and I've got to get this right, I think I can get that right, but the currencies, the corporate bonds sort of thing, let's see how it comes out."

We've lost that sense of delivering certainty in a highly uncertain world because we're experts with access to information which ordinary people in the street just don't get. What I worry about right now is that they are taking risks in order to return the world back to what they would like. That's a big question. Those old rules that we understood worked in a financial market context have now gone. And that's what I struggle with, every single day; I simply don't know the answer.

LG: If you were writing a book, would it be called irrational pessimism?

SC: Well it goes back to the thing about catastrophising all the time. There doesn't seem to be any middle ground in what we do. You need catastrophic theory to drive what you're doing. So you were asking: why didn't I jump on the momentum trade? I talked to clients about this and they're hugely supportive because they were thinking the same thing as you. How do you explain to your clients the reason I bought that thing that was going up was simply because it was going up?

That's what's so challenging and that's why I say, slightly tongue-in-cheek, "Are we dinosaurs?" We're not. What will happen is the long range gravitational forces in the world will reassert themselves. It's just a question of whether they will reassert themselves in a timeframe which will allow us all to keep our minds. Because we all thought, I included, that at the end of the QE, the taking of the corset off the system, going to an unconstrained evidenced-based approach again, would again heroically take us back to a normality which we understood, which we would then be able to do rational investing. It did not work at all. It's left us all scratching our heads.

The way that I've looked at that is to say, "Look, you're actually better off these days thinking about things on a scenario basis, rather than being highly logical about them." What if I get it right? What if I get it wrong? What are the hybrid cases in between? How does that fit into an overall portfolio for clients? Do not give me all your money. I do not want all your money. Have a range of things, I'm a trusted investment partner, amongst the other things that you do, and we should be satisfied with that at this stage.

LG: Successful investing – is it an art or a science?

SC: It's got to be both. Somebody once said to me is it a gift that you've got. And I said to him I think it is but I'm not totally sure. I can see things in the way markets move that other people can't. But then again, the scientist in me says how

213

much of that has been evolution, that you've actually been riding a wave that you were not aware of?

Look, I'm a musician. I play four or five instruments. You don't get to do that, to play in a symphony orchestra, by just playing once a week. You do your two or three hours a day. When I was 15, I was playing five hours a day. I met astonishingly talented people who were at the Menuhin school, and I know people who are very successful professional musicians as well. Everyone was talented but they worked really, really hard as well. They had motivation. There was something in them that needed to come out. They had to work hard at puncturing that membrane to get through to the other side and then it became whatever it was, a connection between soul and intellect and it came out of your fingers, your hands, and how you express yourself. Every muscle toned like we go to the gym. And you get the same doing this job as well, the same with many professional jobs. You do go through this membrane at some point where it becomes instinctive and reflexive.

Chapter 15

The Two Pauls

Paul Causer & Paul Read interviewed by Jane Wallace

Paul Causer and Paul Read have been joined at the hip in their roles as joint heads of fixed interest at Invesco Perpetual since 2002. They have been making investment decisions together since 1995, and are a rarity in being joint managers across around £30 billion of fixed income assets. Read suggests there is actually very little difference between their fixed income strategy and that of equity fund managers. "I'm definitely not interested in chasing a few basis points," he says. "You get performance by getting the big things right over a long period of time."

Jane Wallace: You've worked together for over twenty years now. How did it start?

Paul Causer: I joined Perpetual in May 1994 and Paul came in to get the venture going in February 1995. Before that we worked in different places but we did know each other through business. He worked on the broking and sell sides at UBS and Merrill Lynch and I was with a Japanese bank.

Paul Read: When I joined, I knew that we'd be working together and it was a start-up. I didn't have a clue about how successful we might make it. But what was cool was that there was no fixed income, there was nothing. The chance to run something from the beginning was really interesting – and at Perpetual, which was a quality name. If you didn't screw it up, you had a relatively high probability of it being a success. It was a great opportunity.

PC: Perpetual was an equity house which Martyn Arbib had started off as a kind of a hobby/profession in international equities. By the time we arrived, the PEP market had got going. That was a catalyst for running equities for retail but it hadn't really got going in fixed income. We didn't have any vision about it at that time but it was sort of there. Other than the money fund, the first product we launched was called PEP Bond and it was one of the very early corporate bond funds in 1995.

JW: You've worked together for a very long time, do you tend to get treated as a single person?

PC: Yes to the last one. [Laughs.] It has been 20 years.

PR: More than 20 years.

JW: And do you get treated as a single individual?

PR: To some extent.

JW: Is that really annoying?

PR: Yes.

PC: It doesn't help having the same Christian name.

PR: You shouldn't have hired a guy named Paul.

PC: That's right. Being the first one in, I should have insisted that you use your middle name.

JW: Do you annoy each other?

PR: Yes.

JW: But is that not good?

PR: It probably is good. It's probably ultimately a good thing.

JW: You've got two brains rather than one.

PR: Let's not get too poetic about it but, yes, it probably helps.

PC: In the early days, when you're starting something, it sort of works. And later on, operating in the corporate environment, when Perpetual was acquired and then Invesco went through a tremendous amount of change. It helps to have two.

PR: You've got lots of times when you've got to have someone out of the office and it's good that you've got bases covered. Particularly in periods when the market is difficult, you at least know one of us is going to be looking at it.

JW: Did you always want to be a fund manager?

PC: No.

JW: So how did you get into working at Asahi Bank?

PC: At that time, I was just getting over realising that I wasn't good enough to be a journalist. I'd started working for the *Islington News*, not full-time, but I really thought that was where I was going. But it didn't work out. It didn't help that I couldn't write or spell.

I was an LSE graduate. We're talking about 1984 and 1985, when the City was just getting going and it was becoming more international. There was a ton of jobs for an economics graduate. So I went in as a credit guy.

The first thing I did was pore through documentation on all the restructuring of the big syndicated loans that were given to Brazil and Argentina. The bank itself was going through a number of changes so I ended up managing money and buying securities on a proprietary basis. I got involved in lots of different markets, including gilts, which swung it for me with Martyn. Because all the other stuff I did there, I had no idea what I was talking about. "But do you have any

218

experience with the gilt market?" Martyn asked and I could say, "Yes, I do".

JW: Paul Read, you're from Toronto originally. What attracted you to fund management?

PR: I came to the UK thinking I'd stay for a year. I thought I'd go to law school; I didn't know what I was going to do. I worked in the City and thought it was interesting – there was a lot going on. I did a business degree and got hired by an investment bank from that without really having a clue about anything. If I'd got hired in equities, I'd have been an equity salesman or something. Who knows? It didn't take too long to figure out that – for me, anyway – the long-term interesting bit was going to be managing money.

JW: Are equity and fixed income investing are very different?

PR: There's not a huge difference between fixed income and equity investment if it's done properly.

JW: Not just chasing a few basis points?

PR: No, I'm definitely not interested in chasing a few basis points. That's not the long-term way to get performance in fixed income, in my opinion. You get performance by getting the big things right over a long period of time. Which is more or less what we've been able to do.

JW: What's an example of that?

PR: Not panicking out of markets in 1998 and using it as an opportunity to add risk. Not being contrarian for the sake of it, but trying to look at markets for a contrarian viewpoint, particularly with respect to valuation. There are commonalities. Probably it would be unfair to the equity guys to say they are more interested in the story. Maybe there's a bit more sentiment, a little less maths involved in the valuation. In fixed income, you know what you're going to get. But to be successful, you have to share the same mindset: buying value.

JW: How important is the qualitative analysis then when you see a company?

PC: You really do have to know the company and understand how it may evolve, particularly leveraged companies. So probably 90% of it is quantitative analysis and there's 10% – in some cases, it might be more than 10% – when it becomes instinct. Then it's about what you think of the story and the managers and exactly the same thing that the equity guys would say.

Our business covers more or less every corner of the fixed income markets. In some areas, we get to know companies so well. And when they start to get a bit distressed, maybe coming at them from the fixed income side can give you a better insight to the whole picture than just coming from the equity side.

JW: How do you put a portfolio together?

PC: We don't manage money to a set of risk parameters around an index. So we're not benchmarked. But whether we're looking at it or not, it's a reference point for everybody, so it sort of does matter. If nothing else, it gives a definition of the investment universe.

There's more of a focus on absolute risk and return. I think that comes from the way we built the business, which is more retail rather than institutional. So within degrees you can get the mandate and use it a little bit wider and offer more flexibility. Our approach is to use that flexibility as much as we can.

JW: How important are interest rate movements in today's world?

PC: Hugely. The economists would call them policy rates these days and they really do extend through quantitative easing to target other rates. But even when it was just policy rates being used as a tool, they used to set the structure of interest rates. They would call it a risk-free curve, which is actually the foundation for every commercial lending and borrowing rate out there, including what you and I would borrow for a car loan. Certainly all the yields on all the variety of bonds have that.

The market is always trying to work out when they may or may not change, so you're still getting moves based on the belief that interest rates will rise or go lower, even if they're not moving at all.

We just happen to have gone through the most unusual period where we haven't seen an interest rate go up for six years in the UK, longer in the US. Maybe we've got used to them not moving, but we're probably due one any time soon.

JW: As a manager, how important is predicting interest rate movements? Or can you just build portfolios which will cushion you?

PC: I don't like the word prediction. That's something for Nostradamus. We're trying to get a view, get which way the wind will blow – because that's all you need. You don't need to know what interest rates will be this time next year. What you need to know is which way they're going to move next and within what time period it's going to start. It's about reducing the odds, in a way.

JW: Is it harder to run money now than 20 years ago because you have so much more under management?

PR: Yes and no. As I said, I think it's important to get the big things correct and not just try to pick up basis points every day. In the long term, that's not how you make something work. So as long as you have markets that are relatively scalable, I don't think it should be a vast impediment to performance.

I also think that, once you have size, it opens doors for you. You get paid more attention. If you want to see management, management comes to see you, or is more likely to come to see you than somebody who is managing £50 million.

Another difference is that we can now be one of a company's biggest lenders because we can take quite significant positions in its debt. We could end up owning a chunk of them. If it gets worse, and we have to do a debt-for-equity swap and take the company over, we could become a big shareholder. We've done that in the past as well.

Scale also gets you the ability to have analysts and resources and PR people and all kinds of stuff. So there's some downside to it!

JW: There is a lot of discussion about whether we are on the brink of a bond market meltdown as quantitative easing gets scaled back. Do you agree?

PC: No. This is going back to Nostradamus but my guess is no matter how this plays out, it's not going to be as bad as 2008 and 2009. Then it looked for a while like everything was out of control: the authorities were struggling to get to grips with it, there were systemic problems all over the place. It seemed like every weekend we didn't know if a bank was going to open again on the Monday. We're not going to face that.

This is about a policy change. If it starts to happen, it's probably going to be over a period and the authorities are probably going to control it more. They'll move in a more measured way. That's not to say it can't be a source of volatility but I attach a very low probability to it being a complete meltdown.

However, it's still a relevant question because policy was designed to compress yields, to compress the risk-free rate. But remember they were compressing from a higher level. When it changes, I don't think there's any expectation they go back.

So the change is perhaps the range. We got used to base rates in the fives and sixes. It's beyond belief that the next interest rate cycle would be that. You might get a cycle that takes base rates from 0.5% to 2.5% or 3%, with the same kind of thing in the US. And it's probably going to be over a period of time.

The markets will have to adjust and for bond investors it will be a bear market dynamic, for sure. But it doesn't have to be dramatic, it's going to depend on how much, how soon. And there's big question marks over that.

PR: Essentially I agree. It's possible that the central banks get behind the curve. QE has got to have unintended consequences: asset prices have been kind of manipulated. There's always tail risk with any market, so there's some tail risk that we don't even know. You can say we've had a 30-year bull market in fixed income which is at or near its end – it's been a borrower's market for several years. Right now, it's way more interesting to be the chief financial officer at a big company going "look at what I get to borrow at!" than to be the fund manager buying his bonds.

Now the great thing about this is that we could have a great opportunity in fixed income in a year or two, I don't know how long. We have had a huge amount of issuance of high quality paper with low coupons that doesn't give you much cushion to changes in interest rates. So we could have big price movements. It won't be a credit problem. If anything, it makes the credit decision even easier because you could be buying bonds in the 70s, 60s, because the coupons are so low, and they owe you 100.

I think there could be some interesting opportunities coming out of it. We have to get out of this QE mess first but I don't think it's going to be like 2007 through to 2009. It doesn't get a lot worse than that.

JW: What other investors or fund managers do you admire?

PC: Consistency is a good thing but fund managers tend to excel in moments of time and then they become famous. I suppose Warren Buffett is the one, but even he is a different animal these days. He's always there to rescue things. We quite like that, that's our kind of fund manager. Because all the things we were talking about – the fallen angel, the thing that's gone wrong but we think it can come back and it's scalable – is like a mini-Buffett approach.

I also like managers who have gone against the grain or with a huge amount of conviction, even though people are saying that they're wrong. We've been in moments like that. I think we're good at conviction. When everybody hated financials, people inside this company as well as outside, we stuck to our guns.

John Paulson, the hedge fund manager, was like that. He was going against the grain with sub-prime debt. He was selling it and using credit default swaps to try and put on a short. It went wrong, and wrong, and then he made a ton of money for himself and his clients. He almost folded a number of times on the way, but he had conviction.

PR: In our markets, you've got some really thoughtful people like Jeremy Grantham at GMO. And Jeffrey Gundlach at Double Line is very clever. There's a tremendous number of smart people out there.

JW: Do you admire them because they are clever or because they have conviction?

PR: All of that and the ability to be contrarian, the ability to hold nerve, both in a risk-on and risk-off sense. A willingness to wait as well; to be patient.

JW: What do you do in your time off?

PC: Sleep.

PR: I guess I stay fit, do some jogging, that's about the extent of it.

JW: Does that help with fund management? Are there any

parallels between running and investing money?

PR: I don't know what the parallels are because I'm sure there are a lot of very unfit people who are very good fund managers. You don't have to be fit to be a good fund manager.

PC: We're in danger of coming to the conclusion that our joint success is built on his running!

JW: Can we talk about risk? What have you learned about it in the last 20 years?

PC: Risk is everything. Sometimes you have to speak in a way that suggests we are risk managers, but I think all fund managers are risk takers. This is why I don't like prediction because there's too much uncertainty. You're foolish if you believe that you can master it, either with a model or your own ability.

Risk is danger and I think I have a more heightened sense of market danger than I did when I started. There's always something that comes out of left field that you don't foresee. That's the world – it's life as well. It applies to everything: we're all risk takers, risk is everywhere.

I like being engaged in the process of reducing the odds, but knowing I'll probably never reduce them as much as I think I do. You're an idiot if you think you've reduced them down to the minimal, in anything.

JW: Is that what's good about being a fund manager?

PC: Yes. Like lots of other people in all walks of life, you're engaged in trying to contain risk, to be able to make decisions within it and win more than you lose. Trying to eradicate losing, getting things wrong, but all you need to do to be successful is win more often. Or get a few things right or nearly right, more than you get things wrong or nearly wrong.

It's never all or nothing. But it can be as well, that's what I mean with the uncertainty. You could have done something that you thought was safe, in your life, or I could have bought something in a portfolio that based on everything I knew, every stone I turned, nevertheless still goes wrong. So how do you mitigate against that? Never have too much of it. And then you're into portfolio diversification and all the other mitigations of risk. It's good, it's enjoyable. That's why we do it, that's why we still do it now.

PR: I'd say similar. There's no money machine. You can't just have a formula or a process that is repeatable and guarantees you to make money without any downside. Those things don't exist.

The one good thing about fund management is you can be an old fund manager. You're almost considered to be a better fund manager if you've survived into your old age, because you're wiser and you know what can happen. Though you have to be careful that doesn't lead you to be too risk averse.

What has also helped us in this business is an appreciation of the fact that it is not an academic exercise. We're managing real people's real money. Particularly if you

228

start a business at a place like Perpetual, where you're out there meeting the intermediaries and the clients, you get a real sense of it.

We grew the business on UK retail money. It's not some big insurance company saying "here's £150 million". It's money coming in every day from hundreds of thousands of unit holders in our funds. Having an appreciation for their risk tolerances and making sure that you do the best you can to (a) do a good job for them and (b) explain the risks to them and what's going on is really important.

INVESTOR TIPS

Don't buy single corporate bonds is the joint advice to investors from veteran bond fund managers Paul Causer and Paul Read, co-heads of fixed income at Invesco Perpetual. Limited upside means holding an individual issue is potentially more risky than generally assumed.

Read says: "Your best case on most bonds is that you get your coupon and your money back. Your worst case is you get zero. With an equity, your worst case is you get zero, but you might make twice your money or even more."

A case in point was Lloyds. Many private investors considered it to be a safe bet being a blue-chip bank. It also had a tasty 6% yield. The financial crisis, however, put paid to that.

"Gordon Brown forces them to buy HBOS and before you know it, the dividend has gone to zero and you've lost a huge amount of capital," warns Read.

This risk can be mitigated by diversifying over a range of bonds – possibly up to 30. But because there are minimum subscriptions in some cases, you might need up to £3 million to create a proper portfolio, according to Read. Most investors, therefore, are better off in pooled bond funds.

"Bond risk tends to be overlooked by investors when debt is issued by a well-known brand," adds Causer. Name recognition can lull investors into a false sense of security and encourages them to park and forget the investment – while they continue to monitor the "higher risk" equity price movements.

"You have to be careful with credit. You're buying it to get that incremental yield and you may not understand the incremental risk," says Causer.

Chapter 16

All Else is Never the Same

Richard Woolnough interviewed by Lawrence Gosling

Richard Woolnough has been at M&G since 2004 and runs the Optimal Income, Corporate Bond and Strategic Bond funds. Previous to M&G, he was a fund manager at Old Mutual having joined that firm in 1995. He had an interest in economics going back to when he was at secondary school and studied the subject. He sees part of the role of fund management as being akin to economics in action. "I enjoy economics," he says, "I used to think I'm a practising economist."

Lawrence Gosling: How did you start?

Richard Woolnough: I think that I always had an interest in economics. At school we could do economics as an O-level. I had a very, very good economics teacher. Growing up in the 1970s, the economic news was generally the first bit of information you'd see that came on after children's programmes finished. All the way through the '70s. In many ways, it was more dramatic than the economic things that are happening at the moment; the depths of recession and the depths of unemployment. It was the environment you lived in. It sounds like economics theory, but if you've have something that you enjoy, that you are very good at, that takes very little effort, then the output from those three things – as an economist – might be that you do more of it. I could easily, relatively versus the other subjects I was doing, get a higher grade and enjoy the subject more and put in less work. So that was it.

LG: Did you make any connection between the economics and the politics?

RW: I was into politics as well, they're highly intertwined. Politics then was very dramatic as well; governments were changing regularly as opposed to now. You had a lot more dramatic changes. You've got to bear in mind at the time, there was no other media. It's not like now there's other media that distract you; then there were three TV channels. On Sunday afternoon all that was available to watch on television was 'The Money Programme'.

LG: When did it move from being really interested and studying the economics into realising there was a connection with managing other people's money?

RW: When you get to finish at university, you've got a choice of what you want to do. At the time unemployment was high, there was a recession, so I went through various iterations of things that I could possibly do. I would probably have been quite likely to end up down the accounting route because that was more of the career that I could see. Then fortunately I saw an advertisement for a job that was related to the City and so that's where I ended up.

LG: What was the first firm you worked for?

RW: I worked for Lloyds Merchant Bank. I started recognising the links between economics and asset prices. I'm not a natural salesman so asking people to do things or persuade them to do things is not my cup of tea. I got into fund management and that's been the mainstay of my career ever since.

LG: You said at the outset that economics is quite subjective.

RW: I think there's a huge degree of subjectivity. A classic thing is economists always use the words *ceteris paribus* – all else being the same – and obviously that does work, but also all else is never the same. It can be exactly the same, about the same, or it can be very, very different. It's not just a question of what you think; you've got to understand what other people are thinking, what other people's opinions are, what other people's thoughts are. Try and work out how much information is new and how much is old.

A lot of economic theory and economic literature is all about explaining the past. Because then you get the right answer. But trying to look forward is a little bit more difficult. Some people tell you that you can't and it's a waste of time. But I think you can get a vague idea of the direction you're going in and you can get a vague idea of what everyone else is expecting to happen and from that hopefully you can add some intuition.

LG: Is intuition a function of purely experience of being in the market?

RW: I think it's a mixture of things. It's like anything, playing the violin or running or kicking a football, the more hours you practise, hopefully…

LG: The luckier you get?

RW: The better you get. Or the luckier you get, as the case may be. One of the areas I was stronger at in maths at school was probability. That is a science – probability. You know what an asset's going to be and it's taking what's likely to happen and what are the potential outcomes and marrying that with some economic and political thought and seeing the context it sits in. That gives you an idea of where things might happen. Our job is to think forward. There will be mistakes; you get things wrong and you get things right all the time. It just getting the weights relatively correct and that's what we try to do.

LG: Are you conscious of formative events, decisions, or people that you worked with?

RW: It's a mixture of people you work with over the years, and a mixture of markets you've experienced. I was primarily an equity fund manager with some corporate bonds for five years. If I was investing in an equity, I would tend to be biased towards the competitive advantage as a starting point. Industries tended to be more national than they are now. Then it was all localised markets still. Secondly, I would always think about what the exchange rate implications were for companies' earnings because the exchange rate dominates. That will be different from the typical fund manager who tends to think of the earnings, very clinically about what's going on in the business and not thinking about the wider macro spectrum in terms of the exchange rate and things like that.

LG: When did you arrive at the balance between understanding the macro, and thinking through the consequences to make better investment decisions?

RW: It's like I said about my investment approach, we always think about the macro first and then we work our way down. Whenever we have anybody we're training up, and we want them to look at ideas for us, we don't want them to give us a great big macro idea. They are welcome to, and we talk about it, but we're more likely to start implementing things in our portfolios directly where there's that trading anomaly.

You start by developing a micro then you work up from there and think about a sector. There are times the two do coincide, so you have a macro view that coincides with a sector view. So it works in both directions. Some people just go with the macro view, some go with the micro view, I'm very much an all-rounder so I will take every bit of information I can to construct my portfolio. At times, the macro view will be really important, at times the micro view will be. You can't have a set style; your style has to change as the economic environment changes.

If you go skiing and you say to yourself I'm going to go down the slope at the same pace, every day, no matter what the conditions. That sounds like a logical economic scientific thing to do. In reality, some days you want to go down in a minute, some days you don't want to be on the slope at all. On average you'll be travelling down at two minutes 30 seconds or whatever it might be.

It's the same when you look at investment. Certain things are more important than others and you've got to look at those all the time. That's what we try to do; we try to look at all those variables and at times it becomes dominated by one large event, like the banking crisis, but then there's lots of small events that cause that large event. If you spot each small event as it approaches, then when the big event happens, you aren't sat there saying, "What am I going to do?" or "What happened?" or "What am I going to do today?" You're in a position where you've got hurt but not hurt like everybody else. You can think about what the next thing that's going to happen is, as opposed to sorting out the problem today.

LG: Is that about having confidence in yourself and the team and the process?

RW: It's a mixture of things. On a day-to-day basis, it's an analyst pointing out that there are weaknesses in the financial system; so our analysts were pointing out the weakest links which at the time were the Icelandic and the Irish banking systems. They were essentially weak. Secondly is just understanding that there's a bubble in the housing market; now everybody looks back and talks about it but at the time they didn't. It's an understanding of the factors like how important the oil price is in generating recessions, which people even now forget. The oil price has been a very big driver of recession. People forget that all the time and blame it on something else.

In the financial crisis, there were lots of bonds that were issued that said "We're going to call these bonds but if we don't call them you get this new coupon", so they were at different variable redemption dates. We looked at those and I had conversations where people said, "Yes, they're going to call them – they're going to call these bonds on these dates". So I'd say why are they going to buy these bonds back in 2009, why don't they just roll them instead? The answer was: "Because they have to, because it's the moral thing to do; because it's convention; because it will close their funding off". So the general principle was that these bonds would be called.

But I prefer to stick to the letter of the law and look at legal documents. There had been examples before. Back in the '80s they issued these bonds and these issued bonds were called and they were rolled over at very low effective rates. And so they have done it before. You point that out and they say, "Well, that's a different era, different generation".

LG: In scenarios like that, did you feel like you were being contrarian?

RW: Sometimes you do these things and you think that you see something and nobody else can see it. That's odd. You start questioning yourself. But once you've got there, you then make the next decision. What are the risk-rewards? So I see this but does that mean I'll do really well out of this? What's the extra yield I'm giving up on what I'm buying instead? All those kinds of things.

Obviously we didn't think that the financial crisis would be as awful as it was. But as you got to each step, then you got there and because you were the right side of the transaction, you could say, "Actually, I don't know where the next step is, but the next step is it's going to get worse".

Sometimes the principle you have doesn't disappear. The best example of that is that I believe in the mixed economy and I believe that exchange rates exist for a sensible political and economic reason. I was a fund manager in 1992 when we left the ERM, and I remember having a conversation with somebody about that when it was happening. That was quite interesting. "It can't happen, it can't happen – no, these are the rules." It is these rules – 90% of the time they're right, but 10% of the time they're wrong, which will be painful. On risk-reward, at certain times you want to be – not contrarian – but you want to have the right view, not a different view, you're always aiming for the right view.

Exchange rates need to move. All the way through into the financial crisis and post-crisis, where we are now, I have the underlying belief that a single exchange rate is not an effective economic currency pool. I don't know when it's going to fall apart, I don't know which ones are going to go off, I don't know if it's going to be this year, next year, 100 years, 200 years, I don't know when it's going to happen. But I know that economically, it causes some dislocation because the most efficient way to move the price of labour and goods around is through a free, floating exchange rate. And the free, floating exchange rate has been abolished in the eurozone, so there should be some economic consequences of this. I don't know what they're going to be.

I have been very impressed and very surprised about how the eurozone has stuck through this crisis. In Italy, Spain, Portugal, even Greece to an extent, they've got through it. Maybe I'm sceptical and will be proved wrong and politics will win over the economics, but if you've got a long-haul view about efficient use of capital or economic model, you stick with that and you know that eventually you're going to be right.

LG: Do you think it's got harder due to the growth of the media?

RW: I think it makes it more interesting. You've got more data than you ever had before. That can help and direct you so you can become more efficient. At the same time, it means you can use the data to create and extrapolate things that aren't correct. I think the more information you have the better, I think it's good for all market economics. The more information you have about something, the more efficient you're going to be about allocating your labour and your time.

But people then become more short term. For example, I don't bet on the horses, but you look at the racing pages and it's got a number of data there to make you believe you can make a right decision. It will have like the best form, course and distance, there will lots of tips around, lots of data around there. At the same time, you try and play a fruit machine, the fruit machine will have lots of ways to make you think you're influencing the outcome. But you don't influence the outcome. It's giving an image of control over the process and the outcome but you're still going to put £1,000 in and get £800 out. That's it, because that's what the computer does. But you think you're controlling all that. It's designed to do that.

If I'm able to look at all that noise coming in and ignore it and get some true resemblance of what the true payout is, then the more noise there is, the more people get confused by the noise, then the better it is for me.

Sometimes you think I'm not contrarian but when you think something is really, really cheap and somebody tells you it's very, very dear, then you think, "Hmm, that's interesting".

An example of that would be quantitative easing. At the same time they announced QE, the stock market was very, very low. They announce QE right at the bottom of the market because they're really scared the world is going to fall apart. And it doesn't fall apart. The stock market goes through the roof and they close QE and think everything is fine now, we don't need to do this policy measure.

You can see the causal relationship and you can plot it. But isn't it just the central banks just reacting late? Announcing QE when the markets in a trough and finishing it now when everything is okay? Are central banks making the same mistake as other people sometimes make in that they're looking at today's data and take that as where we're going as opposed to looking at where tomorrow's data is going to be?

LG: How do you learn from an investment mistake?

RW: You have to just move on and try to live with it – you could have done better or you should have done better and you've got to live with it and start looking forward. You've got to keep looking forward and stop looking back.

LG: Are you conscious of a pressure on you as an individual?

RW: You come in and you sit down, like everybody else you sit down at your desk, switch your computer on, do your job, switch off, go home. Obviously whether you're running a small fund or a large fund, you're always thinking about it, on the way in to work, at the weekends, always thinking about what's going on, at the back of your mind, something is ticking along about what's going on in your portfolio.

LG: Is that because you really enjoy it so much?

RW: I enjoy economics. I used to think I'm a practising economist. So all the other economists write about stuff. I'm very fortunate in that not only do I write about it, bits and pieces, but my thing is actually trying to implement that in the portfolio. At the end of the day, I have a job that's about allocating assets at various different terms. I think about interest rates all the time and think about currencies all the time, I think about different sectors, different corporations. So that's what I want to do. Hopefully I can take that and use that in a practical real world situation as opposed to the theoretical world. That's what drives what I try to do and I think the other guys try to do in our funds as well.

LG: So when you meet somebody on holiday?

RW: I usually say I manage corporate bonds. At which point obviously, I get "What is a corporate bond?" I say, "Well, say, Marks & Spencer wants to borrow some money for 10 years like you want to borrow money for a mortgage for your house or a car, and we just lend them the money and that's it." That usually stops them.

LG: Are you conscious of how many thousands of individual investors, policy holders, you're managing money on behalf of?

RW: Yes, it's interesting because by definition, for various reasons, you get removed from them. There's a specialisation, a division of labour, so we have other people who speak to investors. Secondly, compliance-wise, it's really difficult. You're not allowed to speak to anybody. There is this wall that's got bigger. When the funds are smaller, you get nearer to people.

But the responsibility is to do the remit they give us, so we have different remits, some of them more conservative, some of them more ambitious, more free-ranging. That's what we have to do. We sit there and we do the best, whether it's a large investor or small, I'm doing the same thing for the portfolio. That's what we're trying to do. If people give us money and they just want an absolute return with no risk, we will produce an absolute return for them with no risk. That's what the marketing wants to hear, that's what the client wants to hear, that's what the IFA wants to hear. But as a practical economist, I don't think that's necessarily available. So in order to earn a return, you have to take a risk and that risk should be in my world mainly about taking duration risk, interest rate risk, and mainly about taking credit risk and trying to work out which to take. That's what we do, whether it is an institutional client or a retail client where they have £1,000 with us.

LG: How do you feel when the clients put more money in when you're not necessarily as positive about opportunities out there, or the reverse, take money out?

RW: My view is it's their money. It's their responsibility. Our responsibility is to manage it correctly when it's here. But it's an economic decision like any other. People have got to decide what they wish to do with their money, whether they want to be conservative with it, whether they want to run a balanced portfolio that's partly bonds and equities, whether they want to go for maximum returns.

I think people save for two reasons. People save just because they want something to fall back on and they want to have a good return as well. So we do two functions and they've got to work out how much risk they want to take to the downside, what sort of assets to buy. They've got to work out how much they want in return by taking risk elsewhere. So that's their decision. If they do that, they've got to speak to an adviser or think for themselves how to do it.

I think one of the things that's really changed over the last 15 years is that when I used to go and see IFAs, the gap in terms of knowledge of bonds would be exceptionally wide. Corporate bonds were only started in 1994 so who was going to be up to speed in 1997? But they're getting there. The IFAs are understanding – their skill set has improved a great deal, because they've learnt. And I think discretionary fund managers have also learnt and I think the man in the street will learn.

So in places like Europe and the US, people who have a natural desire to save as opposed to speculate, those people understand bonds and over time they'll get to understand what's here. Like they've got to understand equities, they'll get to understand bonds. That means that the market can be more developed and more interesting than it was before because people will hopefully understand from owning a bond for a while, or seeing the interest price, or seeing what drives the valuations round, they understand how it works.

People will learn things. There'll be examples when things go well and there'll be examples where things go bad. Let's say there'll be some bond issued that's just issued purely to retail with no institutional investors, a very small bond deal. You're going to get that kind of small deal with a high headline yield and people will flock to the high headline yield. So there might be some issues because those things tend to sit outside compensation schemes. Admittedly those kind of things can happen, it's happened to equities before, it's happened to property before and at some point, as has happened in other parts of the world, it might happen to bonds as well. I hope it will be limited in its nature. But that's why hopefully people continue to use somebody who reads documents, goes through things and understands what they are.

I think there has been that change in the dynamic over the years as people do know more about bonds than they used to and hopefully M&G, before my time, were quite involved in educating people when they first had a corporate bond fund and hopefully people realise that's how it works, that's what it does.

LG: When somebody says to you why use an active fund manager, active fund managers are expensive, what is your response to that?

RW: There's a mixture of points. There's an element of yes, why not run your own investments. The other point is why use an ETF, you can do it yourself. You do other things, you book your own travel insurance, car insurance, check yourself out of Sainsbury. You have all these skill sets that people used to do for you, so there's an element of that. I think it's a case of the more sophisticated investor you are, the more relaxed you are about doing that, the more comfortable you are with taking risk.

One of the problems with a lot of trackers is you identify the tracker after the event. That asset allocation we talked about at the start is very, very important. In terms of equities, the danger becomes if everybody starts thinking that way, you get an almighty dislocation. Because if everybody starts doing things because it's in an index, then the fundamental question becomes why did you buy that? I bought that because it was in the index. There is no efficient capital allocation involved in that. Index trackers don't always perform as well as the index because of the dislocations that are sometimes involved. It's a lot easier in equity markets to get efficient trackers than I think it is the bond market.

So that's another reason. And again, it means if you're a bad company and you issue lots of debt, then people buy some more. If you're buying it because it's there, then eventually it's an inefficient allocation of capital. So an inefficient allocation of capital does two things; one it makes the economy not work very well and two it costs people money eventually. That's why I think that an index, it's got to be a balance, a balance between some indexing and some non-indexing makes sense. But if you get into pure indexing, you end up in all sorts of distortions.

When one index is doing particularly well, the best example is the tech bubble, that index, everyone wants to pour into that index, or be like that index, everyone wants to buy that particular thing and have 25%, 30%, gains per annum and it all goes into that. Then all these wonderful things come up and everyone wants to buy them and it's like, you're buying it, why are you buying it? You're buying it because it's there and not because you want it.

LG: What do you say if somebody says to you fund managers are overpaid?

RW: I think there's a lot of headline stuff knocked around. It's got to be a function of what they achieve for their business and their clients. Now what do you do when that business is achieving high profits? You've got to work out how you pay that individual and how much of that profit should be attributed – whether it be a footballer or an actor or a director or whatever it might be, a fund manager, what percentage. Should you just cap it because all fund managers should be capped at a fixed level a year? What do you do if you've got a fund manager that's running a large amount and a small amount, how do you differentiate?

There is inefficient allocation of capital, like governments allocate capital, capitalists allocate capital. Governments don't get it right all the time but they generally do a good job. Capitalists don't get it right all the time but they generally do a good job. I think that's the way to think about what's the purpose of anything or any work. And you get into questions of how do you allocate in society and it's very difficult and there's a certain amount of randomness and some is seen as acceptable behaviour because it's socially acceptable, like kicking a ball, and some is seen as socially unacceptable behaviour, like banking. It's a function of a free market.

LG: Do you have one tiny bit of advice or investment wisdom for a private investor?

RW: There are some rules; if something has gone wrong, whenever you sell it, it will be at the bottom. So you either sell it today at 80p, it's the bottom, or you sell it in 3 weeks' time at 40p, that's the bottom. Or you sell it in 10 weeks' time at 20p, it's the bottom. So just recognise that where it is now is the correct price, not where it has been. Don't look back and think this was £4, now it's 50p, it's cheap. Sit back and think, "Would you buy this today?" Take all the emotion out of it, look at it and think, "If I didn't own this, would I do this?" If the answer is no, sell it and do something else.

So the main thing is you can do more with your money, with your life and your time than worrying about individual stock. People should think, if they start looking at their investments on a day-to-day basis, they are no longer investors, they are speculators. It's hard for them to avoid the noise – they'll only ever see bits of noise. They won't bother about their investments and then suddenly they'll get a report that says it's done very well or very badly and this and that, and then they react. They're not seeing noise all the time, it's just one bit and it's usually the noise you don't really want to see.

Chapter 17

The Income Investor

Carl Stick interviewed by Lawrence Gosling

Carl Stick began his career straight out of university at the Tunbridge Wells-based stockbroking firm Neilson Cobbold, before it was snapped up by Rathbones in 1998. In early 2000 he was given the task of managing the firm's Income fund right "on the cusp", as he puts it, of the dotcom market crash.

Lawrence Gosling: So what makes an equity income investor?

Carl Stick: I arrived at it by chance, starting in a research role within Rathbone. We had the small income fund, passed on to me as a way to cut my teeth. It was £9 million, it was tiny and there was no pressure because nobody knew about it. I'm not being flippant, it was important but it was an opportunity to run some money.

You can't overestimate how lucky I was. In terms of timing; to be given an equity income mandate during the TMT bubble because we were on the cusp – if I'd been given it in 1996, I probably wouldn't have been quite so enthused. I'd have had four years of pain. As it was, I started running it in

2000 and 15 months later the market had collapsed and amazingly enough the stocks that I'd been investing in, cash generative, high-yielding old business models, did very well.

The second massive piece of good fortune was the fact that it was a time when nobody was taking a blind bit of notice of it. It meant I could work out how I was going to run it without having commercial pressures from people from outside. What mattered was whether or not the dividend or the distribution the fund generated was worth more this year than it was worth last year and whether I was going to be able to raise it next year.

We had a tremendous run, 2000 through to 2007; the fund went up from £9m to £1.3bn. But by the time you get to 2006/2007, there was a definite change. We outperformed every year, we were first quartile every year but you've got to keep on doing it. Then when the market crashed, a lot of the good fortune and the result of that good fortune – the positions that we had – had gone by the time you get to 2007 because you were owning stocks that were too expensive or whose business models were failing. That came back to bite us.

But at least we'd had that run. In that period of time people weren't judging us by what's happening over the next three months, over the next six months. Since then, we've had to reboot ourselves, and ask what were we doing that was correct, what were the mistakes that were made, but at the same time, try and get back that freedom to invest over the longer term. And in a way, the success of the first few years has enabled us now to have the freedom to do that, because at least we can have a narrative with the clients, and say, "Look, this is our aim, to grow the distribution".

If our distribution – the cash our companies generate year in year out – goes up then the total return looks after itself and the best thing we can do is ignore the short term, think about the longer term and if we do that, we can be very successful.

LG: Why have you always seen the distribution as being important?

CS: I come from the private client side where you recognise that people wanted their income cheque to grow. I remember having discussions with private clients who were very attached to certain businesses because of the yield. But it's not just yield, it is the sustainability of that dividend.

Then it was a very short step to recognise when we look at a business, look at the cash that it's generating. For every single business we look at, it is understanding what cash is generated, who is being paid and ultimately what is left to come back to the shareholders. It was that development. That was a very simple, straightforward focal point of the investment process.

It is an equity income fund. The clue is in the name. You can argue total return is important, of course it is. The first book I ever read about investment, about Warren Buffett, he doesn't want income, he wants that money to be reinvested; I totally get that. But I was given an income fund, so I can't say I'm going for total return. It's a discipline that we stick to.

251

LG: How do you differentiate between the higher risk-type businesses that are good yielders from the ones that are lower yielding but you think are more sustainable?

CS: It's just looking at every business separately. They've all got different models, they're all in different markets and the structure of the markets is different. The competitive stresses are different, and it's understanding where the stresses are. You can hold on to the yield, if the business model is breaking, that dividend can be cut, and it's often the right thing to do. But we have to spot that.

It's just making those assessments as to whether or not this is a cheap stock or whether it's a value trap. To what extent are the earnings sustainable, or are they illusory? That's the big part of what we do. Every single business we look at is different and we have to analyse them.

We do look at cash. We look at cash flow coverage of dividends. We try and understand if that starts to deteriorate, or the business is spending too much cash in other directions and the cash coverage for the dividend is getting less and less, that is a warning sign to us. But it's part of the bottom-up analysis

LG: You do describe yourself as a value investor. How do you define that?

CS: It's a hard one. I like to think we're value but we do also own stocks that are arguably more expensive. We're not necessarily deep value although we do like the idea about buying a business where people have got the valuation wrong. But in reality, that's not always the case.

I think the valuation side is arguably more on the upside. I think it's going to take another 20 years before people accept that we're going to hold a business across the cycle irrespective of the valuation. That's where we got hurt before. We recognise that if something is too expensive, the shares can come down very quickly, and that does hurt performance and that does have a commercial impact.

So I think when it comes to valuation, obviously we like to buy things when they are cheap and we are very cognizant of the fact that when certain stocks get too expensive, we take the view that we should be reallocating some of that capital to other businesses. Nick Train will take the view that if you think a business is going to double over the next 10 years, why sell it now? And I get it. He has his narrative, he has his method; he explains it to the underlying client and they get it. So there's no turnover.

This is Benjamin Graham's whole point; you buy businesses when they're very cheap. You buy cigar butts. He was able to talk about businesses where they were trading below the value of their inventory in cash. Now that doesn't happen anymore. The market is more efficient. But I think this is still the aim, to try and buy things when they're very cheap.

You draw a line from Benjamin Graham to Warren Buffett; he likes to buy things when they're cheap but he doesn't necessarily buy cheap things now. He buys businesses where he thinks there's that earnings power that's going to last for decades. The compounding effect. So should we be buying businesses that are the latest compounders? Again, not necessarily – you're never going to get them when they're dirt cheap, but you get them when you think, actually, at this entry point, we can make a lot of money over an extended period of time. Is that value investing or is that long-term investing or is that compounding? I don't know how you label it.

LG: It's semantics?

CS: Exactly and I think our argument is we'd rather own the greatest businesses at fair prices. Every so often, when those businesses are too highly valued, we'll buy less good businesses at very cheap prices, but when we're looking at any investment, we're marrying up all these levels of risk. What's the business risk? What's the chance things go wrong? What's the financial risk? And is the price that we are paying the correct price, or commensurate with that risk? And if it gets too expensive, using a Grahamism, if Mr Market wants to offer you the silly price, well then you take advantage of that.

LG: How do you get your investment ideas to start with?

CS: New ideas can come from anywhere and I think there are three principle areas. One is just keep your eyes open. Be observant. A major fault of the professional community is they're so focused on quarterly numbers and the minutiae, they don't actually take a blind bit of notice of what is common sense or obvious. So look and see if is a shop is busy, read books, read papers. A lot of the time, the ideas we've had have just come from a germ of an idea, which isn't rocket science, it's just thinking about things in a straightforward way.

Second, we use some research from outside and every so often you will get a good idea from third parties. But the problem with that is they have their own axes to grind.

And the third thing is using screens, which is focusing on two very simple metrics: return on investor capital and earnings yield, which is just a reflection of how cheap/expensive the stock is. Two very basic ideas, based on a screen developed by a guy called Joel Greenblatt in the States. He's written two great books, *The Little Book that Beats the Market* and the sequel *The Little Book that Still Beats the Market*.

That will throw up new ideas or new themes. I remember three or four years ago it highlighted the value in the aerospace and defence sector… and that led to one of our first recent forays into the overseas market, which was buying Lockheed Martin.

I remember an old colleague of mine, donkey's years ago he was at Heathrow airport, and a colleague was returning home from holiday and bumped into him. And he said, "Hello, where are you off to?" And he said, "I'm not off to anywhere. I'm just observing, I want to see footfall." This was a very, very basic idea of just using your eyes and just seeing what was going on.

So Restaurant Group – Frankie & Benny's; when my children were the age when they used to find that really exciting, we used to go there an awful lot. You'd just see how heaving it was at half-terms, party after party after party of kids there. People were saying really, it's not a very good investment. But they were confusing an investment and a gourmet meal. You can go to massively high-class restaurants in London but they don't last long, because they're not good businesses. The food may be great but there's no longevity. Whereas a Frankie & Benny's – I know the food isn't gourmet but it's consistent, it serves a market and they can repeat and repeat and repeat. That makes it a good investment.

LG: How do you not fall in love with the macro-type idea?

CS: Good question. It's hard. Also, with Restaurant Group our view of it has unavoidably changed. We've owned it for over a decade. When we first bought it, it was city-centre restaurants and the management team had gone in there from Six Continents. It was a turnaround story, the old management were trying to open stores and sites overseas, and they had too many brands.

So we bought it as a turnaround. Seeing these guys, you realise they were phenomenally good operators and really focused on detail. That's the pleasure sometimes of this business, when you see people who are very good at running a business. It is that attention to detail; it's not hot air and grand vision. They know how to source things, and systems, and motivation, all these things. We were very enthused about how the business was run.

Then 2006-2007, people were looking at Restaurant Group no longer as a turnaround story but as a takeout story. So they were valuing it as a potential takeout story and also saying it can keep on growing very, very quickly, let's price in that growth. Expectations then were ahead of reality. So when we bought it, expectations were very low so it was cheap, in 2007 they were very high.

Now I think we did take a little bit of money out but not much, so then when the market crashed in 2008-2009, Restaurant Group's shares got hit. From the share price point of view, that hurts. But when we spoke to the management, they said what really scared them was a ramp-up in unemployment. They were saying that as long as people stay employed, they thought they would keep on eating. They were right because there was a structural change; people don't cook in this country the same way they used to. So while the shares came down, actually the investment story, the business story, remained very robust.

That gave us an opportunity to add to our holding when the shares were very weak. You can take a sort of Nick Train-type point of view with regard to Restaurant Group, you can say, "It's a great business, why get out of it?" Yes, there's going to be volatility but it can grow very, very well.

Now, it's changed again, because it's come through that, the rollout has worked very well, people still keep eating out: they eat out even more. Now you've got a business that's rolling out even more quickly, because they've got brands they can roll out more quickly. There's a danger that the market starts to get over-excited again about this rollout. So they're viewing it now as a growth story. So it changes the view of it as an investment, but as a business it's done everything you want it to do from 2003 to where we are now.

I think there's macro and micro. When it comes to macro, we can have a view but we never think we're going to create a portfolio to reflect our macro view of the world. Because we don't know. Genuinely, we can be absolutely economic geniuses and we're going to get it wrong. All we can do is try and create a portfolio that, on balance of probability, we reckon we're going to benefit from most possible outcomes.

But on a micro level, we can look at each individual business – is this business facing headwinds or tailwinds? Are they able to deal with it? How does it affect the market? Is it reflected in the price?

LG: When you do sell a stock?

CS: It's ongoing review. We do create some price targets we're reassessing every day, always thinking about the valuations. We don't want to be continually tinkering. A ridiculous statement for you, but I would love to do nothing, to have that freedom to say, "Right, we own these businesses, we think they're great compounders and that's it – we're sticking with them." But we can't quite do that, so we have to be very mindful of when stocks are getting a little bit too expensive and reallocate.

But ideally I'd love us to own 40 great businesses that we don't have to worry about day-to-day in terms of how they're running and what could go wrong because we think they're bullet proof. But you can't do that, it's very difficult to do that.

LG: And are there any classic "sell" signs from a business?

CS: Sell discipline is the hardest thing. Anybody can come up with a buy idea, selling is very difficult, especially when you are a value investor. But deterioration of cash flow is the principal one.

We are always trying to refine our sell discipline and I think the key word there is discipline. This is something which, 18 years down the line, we're still working on. We try and keep an eye out for certain signals, understanding the momentum of shares, just recognising that maybe the market is right. If something is happening with the price that we don't yet understand, don't automatically assume that we're right and the market is wrong. So you combine those two ideas, the deterioration of cash flow expectations, but also a decline in share price. Is that a trigger?

The advantage of having more people working with me is that more people question why you own things. There is a great difficulty in that when you do get very close to a business, you have that emotion. What we've been doing over the years is trying as many ways as possible to take the emotion out of what we do. It's very difficult, especially when you're taking a long-term view; it can be very difficult to sell a holding.

Alongside that is also recognising once you've sold it, don't worry about it, it's gone. When we get a sell decision right, people don't necessarily know about it. It no longer appears in the valuations so they don't know that whether we got it right. But it's very obvious when sell discipline has broken down or we make a mistake, because you own something that has gone wrong. Then it's blindingly obvious you made a mistake.

LG: So do you think it's a job where you have to continue to keep learning, either about the market from your own mistakes, to keep delivering the value that your investors need?

CS: You have to keep on learning and it's important that the new people who join us teach us things as well. We did terrifically well in the first six years that I was running the fund. Then 2007 through to 2008 was appalling for us. We realised that we'd got a couple of things wrong. So we evolved. We will still make mistakes and we will learn by those mistakes. The process evolves. You can't be dogmatic and say A, B and C, this is what we do. You have principles that you stick to but it has to evolve.

From a personal point of view, I enjoy fund management. But I don't want to be defined purely by fund management. I like the academic side of it. I do like thinking it through and we have been energised over the last couple of years by really thinking about process. How do we make it more defined and more disciplined? I want to have an academic side to it because otherwise it is just a case of sticking a finger in the air. It's got to be a lot more than that.

LG: But there is an element to good fund management which is what you might call instinct or the value of experience. Can you apportion the academic element and the gut/experience element?

CS: It's difficult to apportion but gut and experience, I think they overlap. I think the gut feel is important but the problem is to a degree you focus on the positive rather than the negative. I think you need to have some set of rules that you follow. It doesn't mean to say those rules can't evolve but I think you have to have a clear method. I think gut instinct is important but it shouldn't be an excuse to break some of the principles that you set out for yourself. When it goes right, you think, "Oh, I'm a genius!" and when it goes wrong, you suddenly wish you'd stuck to your principles.

LG: Your fund went from £9 million to £1.3 billion. Do you feel the pressure of looking after other people's money for them?

CS: I don't think it feels like a pressure. I think we really felt when things went wrong, we really felt responsibility for that. It's interesting speaking to clients since then, especially those who stuck with us all the way through. This isn't a game. I think it's too easy on our side of the fence, especially when you're younger, to think this is great, it's fantastic. It's not. In the end, there is a private individual who wants that income cheque and relies on that capital and you can't lose sight of that responsibility.

Going back to the academic side, I'm happier now that we are rigorous enough in what we do to be able to look people in the eye and say we are doing this to the best of our ability and we're doing it in what we think is the right way. That comes down to having a narrative with the adviser or the client and saying this is how we do it. This comes back down to the short term versus the long term as well.

What would be unforgivable would be if we started off doing other things; then we'd feel the pressure because then you know jolly well that you're messing around with other people's money, you're not doing what you said you were going to do, and that's where you get into a lot of trouble.

LG: What can you learn from some of the investment books?

CS: It's interesting. *Security Analysis* (by Benjamin Graham) I think is just a great thing to dip back into. It's not just what Graham wrote, it's also the introductions to the different sections, written by some amazing people. This is the academic side of me. I think it's always very good to ground yourself in this work. Because things do change, markets change, the nature of the markets change, the businesses change. But the principles he's talking about here don't. They're very specific and you follow them through.

LG: So by re-reading the principles, does that help you put a slightly different perspective on some of the things going on in the market?

CS: Every so often there's something that gets people very excited. "You've got to be involved in this, you've got to be involved in that." No, you don't. Just because the market is getting excited in this particular way, you don't have to be involved in it.

The other one which I haven't got here, it's difficult to get, is Seth Klarman's book *Margin of Safety*, which I think is another bible for value investing. All that basically comes down to is if you believe that something is worth *x*, and you can buy it at a substantial discount, you have a big margin of safety. In a way, you don't have to predict macro, you don't have to predict geopolitics, you don't have to predict any of these things because ultimately you've got such a big margin of safety that you're insuring yourself against so many possible futures.

So if you think something's worth £1 and you can pay 40p for it, in the end, you don't mind whether or not the shares oscillate between 30p and 50p, in the end if it's worth £1, you're going to make a lot of money. That's a nugget when it comes to value investing. You've still got to do an awful lot of work. But when you get it right, that is the thrill because actually you can say we've done the work and we've got it right for the right reason.

Sometimes it can take a long time for it to happen. You've got to have patience. When people say, "Don't own this, it is dead money", actually that could be the right time to own it. You may have to wait a little while but if the market is totally unenthused about something, it might be the time to be buying it.

This book *Capital Account* (*A Money Manager's Reports on a Turbulent Decade*, edited by Edward Chancellor) is very well-thumbed. It's about understanding business cycles. Everything happens in cycles. Looking at a business and recognising that when an industry is doing tremendously well, it sucks in capital, everybody wants to play, everybody wants to get involved, high returns attract capital. That capital comes in, those returns get competed down. And then they go below the cost of capital and you get people losing money. Then they lose more money and suddenly they don't want to play anymore. They sell out. And everybody is at the depth of despond, and they're selling out – and it's at that point in time when actually the returns on capital are starting to pick back up again. Then the new cycle picks up.

It's a very basic idea but when it comes to investing in businesses, too many people forget about it. Every single business, every single industry has some form of cycle. It may be a very shallow cycle, it may be a very obvious cycle, but just understanding that business cycle, that has been fundamental.

And then finally this, *Value Investing from Graham to Buffett and Beyond* (Greenwald et al). Just understanding these basic value techniques, this is a book I can afford to keep on re-reading because I don't do enough analysis myself; I don't get the time to.

And the finally, Berkshire Hathaway's annual investment letters. There's been 50 years of Berkshire Hathaway and at the back they've got some various principles written by Charlie Munger. But he's also talking about how he views Warren Buffett and I think the best point he makes is about patience and it's interesting how Neil Woodford's new fund has got the word patient in it. It's a buzzword. It's that patience, Buffett's willingness to buy something and to be patient with it. The people who make the most money are the ones who invest in a business and stick with it over many, many years.

LG: Are there other fund managers in the industry who you've always admired?

CS: I don't know; it's very difficult to say because I don't really look at what other people are doing as far as the UK is concerned. Within my sector, you've got to look at what Neil Woodford has achieved, which is quite extraordinary. You would look at somebody like Artemis's Adrian Frost as well – the longevity of what they do. They stick to the principles of what they do. I'm actually very proud of the people that I work with who have gone on and done other things. I think when I look at someone like Hugh Yarrow (now at Wise Investment), or the likes of George Viney and Sean Beck who are at Troy.

I don't really spend much time looking at what other people are doing, other than looking overseas. I love the idea of some of these big American value investors who are running closed-ended funds who can just go ahead and do their own thing. That's where patience comes in. With the income fund, I want it to be there for the longevity, to keep on doing what it's doing. And it relies on the people I work with to do it. There's part of me that would love to be an academic. That sounds too arrogant, I'm not that bright. But I love the idea of reading books and learning and I think we've got a team that does that as well. So it's great to be getting these nuggets of information from all these other people, these books. That makes it a fascinating industry to be in.

Chapter 18

The Very Modest Investor

Angus Tulloch interviewed by Jane Wallace

After a number of years in a variety of accountancy roles, Angus Tulloch found his calling in Asian equity, investing initially with Cazenove in Hong Kong. For nearly 30 years, he has been running various Asia-Pacific and emerging markets funds under the Stewart Ivory, First State and now Stewart Investors banners from the heart of the Scottish investment establishment of Edinburgh.

Edinburgh appears a world away from the more exciting economies of emerging markets. Nevertheless, one of the most successful emerging market investors of the last three decades has chosen to make his base there.

For Angus Tulloch, the obligation to travel away from the rain is, he admits, no hardship. But the benefits of Scotland – its culture, history and the advantages of living in a small yet dynamic city – remain an equal draw.

Long-established as a financial centre, Edinburgh's traditional qualities of thrift, hard work and looking after clients impressed Tulloch from an early age and remain with him at Stewart Investors.

"The investment philosophy we aspire to is a common one in Edinburgh. It is a long-only style which focuses on getting to know companies well, considering them as partners and not just pieces of paper to buy and sell," he explains.

A third-generation fund manager, investing appears to run in the Tulloch genes. The young Angus bought his first shares aged ten – having applied some filial pressure first.

Certainly his father piqued his interest, entertaining his son with stories of the 1970s Australian mining boom and the stellar rise and fall of the Rundle twins – two resource businesses which entranced investors at the time. In addition, he would invite North American brokers to stay at the family home, emphasising the importance of developing personal relationships in business. This was a lesson the younger Tulloch also took on board.

Tulloch didn't immediately join the fund management industry. After leaving university, he tried other careers in finance – with a self-admitted lack of success – until he found his feet in London as an investment analyst for stockbrokers Cazenove at the ripe old age of 30.

From then on, Tulloch attributes the trajectory of his career as a series of "lucky breaks".

He recalls: "I became an Asia Pacific specialist in 1980 only because Cazenove couldn't find anyone internally who wanted to join their Hong Kong office and I was desperate for a job in the industry."

Being in the right place at the right time was a factor in the move north later on. Tulloch had decided to return to his Scottish roots and happily Edinburgh-based fund management group Stewart Ivory was looking for an Asian Pacific specialist. Tulloch has now been managing money for almost three decades at the same firm, albeit with a few name changes above the door, the most recent being from First State to Stewart Investors.

The push into emerging markets also happened by chance. First State Investments, the asset management group now owned by Commonwealth Bank of Australia, took over Stewart Ivory in 2000. Keen to exploit the potential of Asia Pacific and emerging markets, First State allocated considerable marketing resources to the strategy, as well as allowing the team to run the business as an "investment-centric" boutique.

Tulloch says: "The Asia Pacific universe has always included developing countries such as Malaysia, the Philippines and Thailand. Providing coverage more widely was a natural extension of what we were already doing."

The spur to the launch of the Global Emerging Markets fund in 1992 was a meeting with some Chilean companies in Santiago. Impressed by their management, Tulloch and team became founding subscribers to the Genesis Chile fund which, at that stage, other than buying shares in London-listed Antofagasta, was the only route to investing in Chile.

An investment in Mexico followed soon after and, with South African and East European markets opening up, it was decided there was sufficient impetus to launch a standalone fund.

Investors were however, a little slower to catch on.

"It wasn't until 1996 that we won our first segregated emerging markets mandate from a US State Teachers retirement fund, which, I am proud to say, remains a client to this day," Tulloch says.

More than 20 years on, the First State Asia Pacific fund and its Asia Pacific Leaders stablemate combined had assets of close to £10 billion at the most recent peaks.

So what is the key to Tulloch's long-term success? When questioned, he modestly attributes it to "a huge amount of luck".

He says: "You could hardly have got the timing better being in these markets for the last 25 years."

However, the reality is that a large amount of number-crunching does take place.

In the past, macro-economic analysis has played the large part in asset allocation for emerging markets for most investors. While Tulloch's approach incorporates top-down views, his focus is very much on bottom-up analysis as companies become increasingly multinational. Unilever is a good example of a firm which makes and sells more products in developing markets than in Europe and the US combined.

He says: "We have always viewed markets as providing headwinds and tailwinds with our primary emphasis being on finding quality companies regardless of their location or stock market listing."

Nonetheless, in politically less-developed countries, and in those nations which are resource-rich, Tulloch says macro influences do play a more important part in the investment process.

For instance, the machinations of President Marcos made the prospect of any investment in the Philippines unviable in the late 1970s and early 1980s while, more recently, Tulloch is wary of domestically-focused Australian companies. The view here is that resource prices (and therefore the Australian dollar) are closely linked.

In terms of company analysis, Tulloch and his team look for firms with a well-motivated and effective leadership, as well as a business franchise with high entry barriers and strong cash generation. It is important for the company's culture to be focused on long-term profit sustainability and growth but it must be combined with a respect for all stakeholders – customers, suppliers, employees and the community – as well as shareholders.

Family-controlled businesses are therefore generally attractive to Tulloch as management's interests are aligned with outside shareholders rather than being focused on an individual's aggrandisement.

"We spend much less time than most modelling earnings projections, and much more time in checking out the company's history and its governance reputation," Tulloch comments.

Governance is now a crucial determinant for whether Tulloch will invest or not. This is understandable as company managements are becoming more aware of their impact on the wider world, encouraged by pressure from shareholders.

Tulloch notes that the First State Asia Pacific Sustainability fund is focused on this area and has actually outperformed his own Asia Pacific funds in certain periods.

"This theme has had a huge influence on my investing," he says. "I often find that companies which take short cuts in one area are probably doing the same in another. Those firms which, say, are indifferent to polluting the environment are quite likely to treat minority shareholders badly too."

Signals to sell

Corporate governance, or the lack of it, also has a hand in when to quit a stock. Tulloch and his team are "ruthless" about selling out of a company when there is a suggestion that either the majority owner or management are dishonest or if they treat minority shareholders unfairly. Consequently the portfolio has little exposure to Korea where the team feels corporate governance is weak.

Consistent failure to deliver without adequate justification is also another reason for disposal.

Other warning signs include "diworsification" from core businesses, acquisition binges, choosing poor partners, unmerited management enrichment, sharp tax practices, questionable board appointments and disregard for environmental and social impact.

Tulloch's team also monitors movements in working capital very carefully. Sales and profits may be growing strongly, but if receivables are growing faster, it could signify trouble ahead.

Tulloch explains: "It could be that the company is stuffing its distribution channel, that is, getting other people to hold stock – possibly on extended credit terms. And, until clients pay up, there isn't any money coming through the door."

Valuation

Valuation is one of the bedrocks of the investment process. The first precept is that "everything has a price", or, in other words, nothing is so cheap that you can buy it regardless.

Russia's Gazprom, for instance, seemed on the surface to be a steal but it was cheap for a reason, Tulloch points out.

"Gazprom always looked impossible to value because you never knew what the government was going to do with it," he says. "When it was made to take over a loss-making newspaper, it didn't look so cheap after all."

The flipside of this theory is the second precept: some stocks are too expensive to own, usually because they have been inflated by sentiment or some other kind of market froth.

Tulloch believes that "there is a price for everything – you have to have some form of pricing discipline". But on that basis, it can be difficult to find opportunities in a bull market. And, once combined with the cheap-for-a-reason stocks, about half the Asia Pacific universe becomes "uninvestible".

Despite these parameters, making the call on valuation is never easy.

Tulloch admits: "What constitutes a reasonable price is a very hard one to judge at the best of times. Certainly the funds, for which I am responsible, would have done better if I had run my winners for longer."

Portfolio structure

Depending on whether the mandate permits the inclusion of small caps, Tulloch has traditionally held between 40 and 100 stocks in any portfolio. As a conviction investor, he prefers the top ten holdings to account for over a third and up to half the overall weighting.

But he believes that there is no definitive approach to portfolio construction as he has seen colleagues with very different structures enjoy equal success. What is important, however, is that the fund manager should have complete freedom to make macro and individual stock decisions within the parameters of the mandate. Moreover, if they consider those parameters to be wrong for the client, they should try to have them changed.

"Split portfolio responsibility and managing money to inappropriate parameters are recipes for unhappiness as well as poor investment performance," Tulloch says.

Risk

The word risk can have many meanings, depending on the investment group. At Stewart Investors, risk is defined as losing client money rather than underperforming a benchmark.

While he admits to playing bridge "irresponsibly", Tulloch himself hates to lose money when investing and toying with other people's savings is not an option. He is also very much aware that being a natural contrarian can bring an element of danger.

"I almost want to do the opposite of what is proposed, just for the sake of it. It does make life difficult for the people who work with me," he confesses.

Concentrating on investing in conservative but innovative owners and managers, who recognise the importance of all their stakeholders, is the most effective risk control, Tulloch maintains.

While the portfolios are geographically, industrially and thematically diversified, there is an advantage to being unconstrained by a benchmark. The team is not obliged to hold any particular stock, sector or country and therefore does not have to compromise on buying low-quality stocks merely to match benchmark weightings.

Influences

Tulloch has worked with many inspiring personalities over the years, several of which proved to have a great influence on him one of whom was fond of using gardening analogies when talking about tending to portfolios.

The source of the herbaceous border analogy was Lord Faringdon, a keen gardener and partner at Cazenove during Tulloch's tenure in the 1980s. He would invariably pre-empt any talk of a successful investment with the phrase "we had a bit of luck" and, conversely, own up to any errors promptly.

"He taught me that it was much better at client presentations to provide a full account of one's mistakes over the review period otherwise a critical trustee or consultant would take vicarious pleasure in pointing them out for you," says Tulloch.

Another mentor at Cazenove was Hon Victor Lampson, the partner to whom Tulloch reported when based in Hong Kong. While his grasp of financial modelling may not have so strong, Lampson (later Lord Killearn) had an exceptional ability to build personal relationships and was a keen judge of character. Tulloch remembers reading a rare set of visit notes relating to a Malaysian tycoon. Lampson interpreted (correctly, as it turned out) from the tycoon's choice of grey Gucci shoes that management's interests were focused elsewhere than the business and recommended against investing in the stock.

Finally, long plane journeys around South East Asia were a good opportunity to pick up tips from other investors. Travelling as a broker analyst, Tulloch often found himself in company with Jeremy Hosking, then an Asian fund manager with GT.

Tulloch says: "He always seemed to home in on what really mattered to a company's future. He was especially aware of the need to align management and families with shareholders' interests, long before this was considered important in the investment world."

Teamwork

Such valuable input from colleagues and peers over the years has perhaps encouraged Tulloch to nurture a team approach to investment rather than promote himself as a star fund manager.

"There is too much focus on individual personalities in our industry," he says. "Successful investment, in my view, is about creating the right dynamics between team members so that they enjoy both contributing to, and leveraging off, each other's ideas."

The other important function of colleagues is to provide research. Running a pooled fund with a minimum of 30 or 40 stocks can involve a huge amount of analysis and a team can share the burden. And, if the team has been together a long time, it is possible to counteract their biases.

Market backdrop

As colleagues have changed over the past 25 years, so too have the markets.

The Asia Pacific universe has expanded to include China, India, Indonesia, Korea and Taiwan. Economic liberalisation, the opening of stock markets to overseas investors and more responsible fiscal and monetary policies has seen the Asia Pacific weighting in the MSCI World Index rise from under 3% in 1988 to over 15% now.

Meanwhile, most of Latin America has emerged from its "lost decade", the Iron Curtain came down in Europe and democracy has replaced Communist or military regimes across most of the developing world.

But there have also been significant downturns. For Tulloch, the Asian financial crisis of the late 1990s was particularly hard work.

Tulloch says: "All we could tell clients was that they would lose less money with us than with other managers. It was grim."

The period after the tech boom was similarly challenging, although this time Tulloch had an inkling of the impending crash. He attended a conference on Asian technology stocks in 2000 and managed to squeeze into the presentation given by Richard Li, the then head of PCCW, a dot.com firm with a runaway share price. There was standing room only.

Tulloch says: "We had seen the receivables going up on the tech stocks but everyone around me had these blank expressions – a sort of semi-adulation. I realised that they didn't understand what was going on. It didn't make sense to us either."

This insight was backed up by what Tulloch was seeing around him on this travels. As he says: "When taxi drivers start talking about stocks and shares, there are hundreds of cranes outside your hotel window and banks are building new headquarters, you know the market is going to tank."

As for the future, Tulloch says: "It would be wrong to assume the generally very benevolent political climate and currency stability of the last 20 years will prevail for another 20 years."

INVESTOR TIPS

Angus Tulloch is highly conscious of the bedazzling effect of the latest investment fashion.

"Beware the wisdom of crowds," he warns. "So often a good economic story does not make for sustainable investment performance."

The prime example of this phenomenon is China. Even after its most recent speculative run, by mid-2015 the MSCI

China index was still below its end-1992 level despite the Chinese economy being one of the fastest growing in the world over this time.

Another aphorism on which Tulloch relies is that "you rarely find one cockroach in a cupboard" or, in other words, one piece of bad news is often followed by others.

A profit warning could indeed be a great buying opportunity if the reason for the downturn is logical – cold weather affecting ice-cream sales, for example. But scepticism is required. It could well be that more serious problems are impacting revenue such as secular change or increased competition.

"The recent share price behaviour of Tesco reflected elements of such seismic changes. However, it was so easy to catch the falling knife while again and again the company disappointed," Tulloch says.

Learning from mistakes – one's own and others' – has also been an aid to successful investment. Stewart Investors encourages an internal culture of owning up to errors and understanding why they happened.

Tulloch says: "It is so much easier to remove a stock from a portfolio when you stop pretending that you haven't succumbed to some irrational emotion or failed to analyse the company properly."

Finally, his advice is to stick to what is easily understandable. Tulloch avoided technology, media and telecoms (TMT) stocks in 2000 and it ended up being a vintage year for the funds in both absolute and relative terms.

"Always focus on quality in terms of owners/managers, franchise and financials. It's not rocket science at all," he says.

Chapter 19

You Can't Ignore China

(a) Andy Rothman interviewed by Lawrence Gosling

Andy Rothman lived in China from the 1980s until 2014. He is now based in United States, working as the investment strategist for Matthews Asia. His prime responsibilities lie in developing China-focused research looking at the ongoing economic and political shifts taking place in the country. Prior to joining Matthews, Rothman spent 14 years as CLSA's China macroeconomic strategist, and before that he spent 17 years with the US diplomatic service based in the US embassy in Beijing. He is a proficient speaker of Mandarin.

LG: When you first went to China as a student, what struck you about the country?

AR: I had no expectations. It was shortly after all the turmoil of the Cultural Revolution and I thought that was just China's version of Woodstock. The US and China re-established diplomatic relations in 1979 and I coincidentally had an economics professor who was Chinese and so he was offered a grant to take some students to China and asked me if I wanted to go. It just sounded like an adventure. Having had the opportunity to go there so long ago has had a big impact on the way I think about China. If you would have asked me 30 years ago will China be a pretty rich, stable country that is a major driver of global economic growth and is a serious part of anybody's investment portfolio, I would have said the chances of that are close to zero. Being wrong for a couple of decades about where China could go or would go has helped in thinking about where it's going now.

LG: Would it be right to describe it as a sort of state form of capitalism these days?

AR: In some ways. I think it's important to recognise that different parts of the economy have evolved at a different speed and some parts of the economy are still struggling. It's not unlike what we see in the UK in that London might be doing fantastically here but there are certain cities in the UK that are struggling, given what their economies have been traditionally based on.

The same is true in China. You've got what I would call the world's best consumer story in China where retail sales are growing, adjusted for inflation, by more than 10%. This is based on 8% real income growth on average for families in China, which is phenomenal, almost no household debt, great optimism about the future. On the other hand, if you go to a handful of provinces where the economy is heavily based on construction-related sectors like steel and cement and aluminium and glass, on resource extraction, oil and gas and coal and iron ore, those places are suffering. Unemployment is higher, growth is slower.

LG: Why is it that people don't see the long term?

AR: Part of it is that China is changing a lot, very rapidly, and there are cultural and political aspects that are hard to understand unless you focus on it. China has become so big that everybody in the financial sector now feels they have to be a China expert. To me it's like if you asked me my opinion on Greece, my initial response would be I'm not really an expert on Greece so I don't have a lot of value to add to that. Whereas I think a lot of people feel now if they get a question on China, they have to answer it.

LG: So when you say long term, you're talking 20, 30, 40 years?

AR: Yes, but it doesn't even have to be that long term. Let me give you an example. The government … has talked in more detail about how it's going to deal with the local government finance issue, where they're going to swap out bank loans, many of which are at a fairly high interest rate, with bonds at a much lower rate. The primary focus of the government is twofold. One, to improve transparency for local government finance, and the second is just to bring down the bar at cost. It's a complicated big programme and so there have been some hiccups as they've started to implement the pilot project.

They've had to change course. This is a good thing. This is the government saying this is a really big complex programme and we're going to be flexible and pragmatic. One of the advantages they have in not having a democracy is that they can do that pretty easily; they don't have an opposition party that's picking it apart. That's the biggest long-term versus short-term idea. If I'm invested in the region or in China for a five-year, ten-year horizon, how focused do I want to be on the day-to-day mechanics of this, other than to say they're adjusting and so they're keeping their eye on the long term and I'm not going to worry about the day-to-day part of the story?

LG: How difficult as an outsider is it to understand some of the policy and thinking of the Communist Party? Do you need to understand it?

AR: Yes, I think you do, just like you need to understand that here. I think from an economics perspective, the Communist Party of China is actually pretty transparent. Not so much on the political side or the foreign policy side but on the economics. They've come out and said, for example, we are not going to do QE. Full stop.

We know from past experience that they know how to do stimulus better than anybody in the world. In 2009, they ran what I think is the biggest Keynesian stimulus programme the world has ever seen. I think they're being pretty transparent about this.

LG: As investors we seem to focus on the quarterly GDP.

AR: Things are changing so much in China. We got used to two decades of 10% growth. It couldn't do anything wrong. That was over-enthusiastic. Now we're often being overly pessimistic because China is only growing at about 7%. I'm always reminding people that because of the base effect, that for a company selling goods and services to Chinese people, you'd rather be operating today than 10 years ago. In 2014, for example, GDP growth in China was 7.4%. A decade before it was 10.1%. But the base on which the 7.4% was multiplied in 2014 was 300% bigger than the base a decade earlier. The growth in China in 2014 in terms of the size of the economy was 100% bigger than it was a decade earlier at the faster growth rate.

LG: The demographics in China are not as favourable as in other parts of the investing world, what's your response to that?

AR: It's a good question. It's also one of the reasons why growth has to be slower because those two decades of 10% growth every year, just the increase in the size of the working age population was responsible for 1 or 2 percentage points of that growth. Now, as you said, the working age population is starting to shrink a little bit so that's a negative drag on growth. But the question is can they meet that challenge of moving up the value chain and becoming more productive and efficient?

I think there's a lot of evidence that they're moving in the right direction. For example, if you go back to the middle of 2005, the Chinese government broke the hard peg between the renminbi and the US dollar. Since that time, the renminbi has appreciated by about 35% against the dollar; that's a lot. It's appreciated more than 50% in real effective terms against all of its major trading partners. Since that time, the minimum wage in Southern China where most of the exports come from has gone up 340%. So a lot. And yet, the share of total imports in the US that comes from China has gone up from 14% to almost 20%.

So that's a pretty strong headwind of expenses, costs, that China has been competing against and the only reason for that obviously is they've moved up the value chain and become more efficient and productive. We can't say for sure that China is going to be successful in this restructuring and rebalancing but I think people are too pessimistic because they're not recognising how much has been done already.

Investment is still by far the biggest share of the Chinese economy but in three of the last four years, including last year, consumption accounted for more growth in China than investment. So that big super tanker, the Chinese economy, is clearly turning around.

LG: Do people misunderstand what the consumption story is?

AR: Well it was never really about Gucci handbags. But this was a sexy story to tell people when China was driving Gucci's profit. But the average Chinese person was not buying a Gucci handbag. Now you've got the world's fastest growing and one of the biggest car markets in the world. You've got home ownership and about 85% of urban families own their own home, probably second only to Singapore. It has really changed because income has gone up and not just for the rich but across the board.

We've been told by too many economists that the only thing that matters is the share of GDP that comes from consumption as opposed to looking at the change. Yet at the same time, we do understand the consumption story because we know that some of the most expensive equities in China are the consumer stocks. We can see that on an investment basis but we're having trouble accepting that on a macro basis.

LG: The macro story about China is one thing, but the stock market is perceived as volatile and that makes investors shy away from Chinese equities?

AR: Yes. I'd look at that in two ways. One is for anybody who's trying to invest, even if you're not investing directly in Chinese equities, or even in Asian equities, China is such a big part of the global economy that you need to know what's going on. China is now about a third of global growth. China contributes more to global growth than the US and Europe combined. So a large part of what I'm trying to accomplish is just to make sure that people realise they need to be educated. They need to be smart about China. Even if they're not going to directly invest. The media is too often focused on the short term and too often on the negative and that might make you afraid of owning [young] brands. You might look at a company that has a significant share of its growth from China and be afraid of that because everybody is telling you that China is collapsing, it has the slowest GDP growth in the last 25 years. But it's 7%. I would say as an investor, stop and say to yourself, "How much of my month do I think about what's happening to global oil prices, or to what's happening in the EU? I should probably apportion that amount of my brain space to think about what's happening in China".

LG: What are the issues that you think people need to be cognisant of when balancing up the risks with the rewards?

AR: I would say that in recent years, when it comes to economics, by and large the Chinese have been very pragmatic and done good stuff. They make mistakes every day but they tend to go back and fix them. Unlike in the United States, there's almost no ideological component to the economic debate in China. Politics however, is far less pragmatic. You have an economy and a society that are increasingly based on private property rights. Most people own their own home, most people work in small privately-owned companies and yet on the other hand, there's no rule of law. There are no institutions that people really trust. Over the long term, that's not sustainable; that has to change.

I'm concerned that there has not been an expansion in the room for political discourse like there has been for economic discourse. So you can sit in Beijing and say, "I think the Chinese economy is collapsing" and you don't have to worry.

But you can't make similar statements about the Communist Party and not worry. That has to change over time.

I'm also concerned that they've been too aggressive in the region on the political security side. As I said before, I think it's positive that they seem to be acknowledging that maybe they've overstepped and they've pulled back a little bit. But I am worried about that. And I'm worried that they're not dealing quickly enough with the environment.

LG: On the personal freedoms that were put in place, were they essentially so the Communist Party could shore up its control? Or was there another more altruistic driver behind it?

AR: I think it's a combination of both. It's the Party saying we saw what happened in the Soviet Union and Eastern Europe and we don't want to end up that way. What can we do to stay in power? If you look at 1989, I think the Party understood that they were not going to survive if they had to send the tanks back out again. I think the lessons they learned from the Soviet Union was that they needed to completely restructure the economy. For example, starting in the mid-90s, they sacked 46 million state sector workers in six years. Yet few of your readers will know that that took place. At the same time they allowed people to set up private companies for the first time. This is a group that's shown themselves over the last few decades to be pragmatic and willing to take pretty big steps to achieve both of those objectives: a wealthier population and stay in power.

LG: What would you say are your top five concerns?

AR: Let me start by talking about what I'm not all that worried about. I think the risks of a hard landing, of a meltdown in the residential property market, of a collapse because of debt – I think these concerns are way overblown. Over the next five years I think the worst we're going to see in China is more volatility and possibly a quarter or two of sub-par growth. The reasons for this are I think the economic fundamentals are pretty good. The government is very pragmatic and has a huge amount of resources to deploy if there's a short-term crisis, as we saw in 2009.

I'm far more worried about the longer-term structural issues, particularly the absence of the rule of law, and the lack of Chinese people's trust in Chinese institutions. Because as China becomes more market-oriented, in the long term, it's going to follow the same patterns that other market economies have always followed, which means occasional recessions. It's not going to happen soon but over time, it will go through the ups and downs that we have in a real market economy. When that happens, you need the social and legal and political infrastructure to smooth that out. China isn't there yet. Then I'm worried that as they want more recognition for their global stature, that they don't overreach, that they don't push too far on their neighbours, that they don't push too far on the US.

LG: Now you're back in the US, how does the US view China?

AR: One of the problems we have in the United States is that I think most people are unaware of the kinds of change that have taken place in China. When I travel around the US and talk to clients or potential clients, to investors in general, every time I give a talk I get a question about ghost cities in China. A lot of this was driven by a TV show that was aired a couple of years ago where they went and visited a city that had what appeared to be a lot of empty buildings and empty streets. I go and I talk to people and explain how there are a few places where there have been some dumb decisions made but, by and large, we have to recognise that the way that China's property market is evolving is just different from here.

LG: So that's the traditional development expansion that's happened in every other major economy?

AR: Right, it's just happening on a bigger scale and at a bigger pace. We have to recognise how the scale works. We know how much infrastructure the Chinese are building. So this town that I talked about going to, Zhengzhou, nobody has heard of this town. The metropolitan area is the size of the Washington DC metropolitan area. They're building a subway, under construction now, that's going to be 125 miles. It's the city where most of the world's iPhones are made but nobody has ever heard of it before. So when you say there's some empty buildings there, it sounds like a terrible story. I think a lot of what I'm doing is trying to educate people that we have to accept the fact that things are different there. Better or worse, we have to look at it but we also don't have to just say it's different so it's bad.

LG: And just finally, why can people not afford to ignore China as an investment?

AR: It's just too big and it's growing too fast.

(b) Dr Chen Jiwu interviewed by Lawrence Gosling

Dr Chen Jiwu is the founder of VStone Capital, based in Shanghai, has over 22 years of investment banking and fund management experience harking back to when he began working with the Chinese state-owned Agricultural Bank.

LG: What attracted you to the investment industry?

Dr Chen: Back in 1994, actually computer science was not very advanced in China and even in the banking system. So when I graduated with a Masters in Computer Science, I was hired to develop a clearing system for the banking sector in China. After my project, I was attracted to the equity market. That's why I was hired by the Agricultural Bank to join as an investment analyst.

LG: How has the equity market in China changed in the last 20 years since you've been analysing companies and now managing money?

Dr Chen: The start of the equity market in China was in 1992 with the then President, Deng Xiaoping. Deng said maybe we could use it as a pilot project to start the equity market. If anything goes wrong, maybe we can just close it and it will not be an issue. However, the market has grown so rapidly and it's hard for anyone to say we have to close it.

LG: What do you think are the common misconceptions that Western investors have about the Chinese equity market?

Dr Chen: Over the past few years, I think people not only misunderstood the equity market in China, people misunderstood the economic situation or misunderstood China as a whole. Over the past 30 years, I think globally there was only one person that truly understood China and unfortunately he passed away. He was Lee Kuan Yew, the President of Singapore.

LG: What did he understand that other people didn't?

Dr Chen: He understood the culture of Chinese people; he understood the history of people. There are two groups now in the West. There is one saying that China is going to collapse very soon. The other group think China is not going to collapse and the most prominent one is the ex-Prime Minister of Australia. That group think China is not going to collapse is because in the last 30 years, the economic growth is very strong and the living standards have been improved dramatically and there are more and more middle class

293

coming up. On that regard, it's quite difficult for China to just collapse.

LG: How long is the long term?

Dr Chen: I think the long term, in terms of cycle, it would be five to ten years. There are actually very interesting data points to watch. For example, the GDP growth has been growing down from the mid-teens in 2012 to now 7%. But at the same time, during the same period, the employment rate has been decreasing dramatically and more importantly, the salary for those people are increasing. So this is quite counter-intuitive. I am always puzzled how come people just look at one figure, GDP, top line. If they analyse the unemployment rate or wage increases, the situation would be clearer. It could be because people are a little bit more emotional and they are not looking through the numbers.

I think now is very important timing in changing the whole economic structure and the government is doing it in a very good manner and very successful so far. Because in the past 15 to 20 years, the Chinese growth is very phenomenal but it's also driven by low lending costs, low labour cost, and also some industry that is polluting the environment, and also driven by strong exports to fund the strong growth.

What happened recently is the lending is becoming a little bit more expensive and salaries have increased. Also in terms of exports, the world cannot take so much exports from China anymore. There is a rigorous reform happening and the government want to focus more on a less environmental-polluting environment and also to upgrade the value added for those industries. No longer producing cheap product, they want to upgrade the content. Also they want to promote domestic consumption as well. That is why I mentioned earlier in the last few years there are rigorous economic reforms happening in China.

China is a very big country and is very complicated. If you look at the coastal area, in terms of economy, they are already of a developed standard. But if you move to the northern part or the inland part, they're in developing mode in terms of industry or development. This is a very complicated issue.

The divergence is very extreme. On the one hand they are firing the rockets to the moon, and they have the most robust high-speed rail system, they have a very developed telecoms system in China. But at the same time, in the rural area, the living standard is not very high. If people just look at one small component, it's just like people try to understand an elephant by holding a leg or the trunk, only seeing a small part.

LG: People talk about corruption or the political system, what is your answer to why they are not as important from the investment perspective?

Dr Chen: Actually anti-corruption is very important to China, and the equity market. The Western world should focus more on the impact or the commitment of the Chinese government in tackling anti-corruption and also, more importantly, the government is letting go a lot of power so that no more approval will be required to improve the efficiency. In my view, the Chinese government is cutting their own arm in sacrifice.

LG: If I'm going to invest in China, why should I invest with an active manager as opposed to a passive one?

Dr Chen: Actually the Chinese economy is undergoing rigorous industry consolidation. For example, some of the weak companies, because they're inefficient, their market share is shrinking and shrinking. But at the same time, another group of companies is growing very fast and the market leader in the sub-sectors after their competition disappears, they are able to grow even faster. This group of companies will sooner or later become a monopoly or oligopoly and that would be very good for stock pickers.

At the same time, in certain industries, the competition is very high, in telecoms and the technology industry. I think in terms of competition, it is only US and Israeli companies that can compete. Otherwise the Chinese companies are already dominating the market. If you are just buying the passive index fund, only investing in the large companies, when the market share drops, those companies are no longer market leaders and then the share price will correct.

So for me, you have to use a top-down approach but you have to be more bottom-up stock specific and active in thinking about who could be the next winner instead of just buying the bigger one.

LG: Why should I invest my money with a fund manager based in China as opposed to somebody who travels in and out once or twice a year?

Dr Chen: There is no way that you can manage money in New York, in London or even in Singapore investing in China, because China is so complicated and a big country. You have to spend 24 hours every day there, spending time with the entrepreneur, spending time with the regulators, with the industry people to understand the latest development. Flying in and out maybe once a month, it's just like the elephant story: you only see a leg of the elephant.

LG: What is the lesson for a UK investor investing in China?

Dr Chen: Don't listen to the people who haven't done deep research or due diligence on the real China situation. For any data point that you observe or you read, you have to think about why and then do further work, particularly for the real meaning of the data point and then make a conclusion out of it. Sometimes things are quite different from what you just interpret from reading the figures.

We have to be a little bit more flexible in applying our thinking process, in understanding a country or a fast-growing economy. I think the philosophy in the Western world is very objective and that impacted me very much. When I make an investment, I always want to be objective, I don't want to be emotional. I want to be more patient and not impacted by the market.

In 2005, there was no high-speed rail train in China. Last year, they have 16,000 kilometres of high-speed rail network in China already, which is the largest in the world. This year there will be more, there will be 4,000 kilometres more; in total it will become 20,000 kilometres.

In 2005 there was no Chinese manufacturer who could make high-precision silicon solar panels. In 2012, China is the largest solar panel manufacturer in the world already. In terms of application of internet and e-commerce, I think China is more advanced in certain areas than in Europe. These are examples that actually everything is changing but there are many, many investment opportunities behind this change.

At the same time, there are some challenges for the China economy as well. As I mentioned earlier, it is not only about the good side of China as at the same time there are some weaknesses as well. Just as like in a glass, you have to look at it from different angles, and balance the risk and reward opportunity on the downside.

Chapter 20

Encouraging the Next Generation of Investing Talent

Nichola Pease interviewed by Jane Wallace

After more than 30 years working within the world of investment and fund management, Nichola Pease, is a founder member and chair of Investment 2020, an initiative which aims to attract a more diverse range of people into fund management.

She is married to Crispin Odey, the hedge fund manager, and she is the brother of Richard Pease, now at Crux Asset Management.

"When I came into the City over 30 years ago, there was a much greater breath of educational bandwidth. There was a view that university gave you time to grow up and to develop your thinking. It didn't matter if you had done a history degree, or classics, or English," she says.

Having held various senior roles at asset management companies since, the young Pease had some misgivings about her career choice in the early days.

She says, "I felt very uncertain. I thought they'd picked the wrong person. But that in a way drove me on to try harder."

Pease attributes her student travel around Uganda rather than her English Literature degree as the reason why Kleinwort Benson hired her. She was one of a group of eight picked from a thousand applications, and one of the first female graduates to join the training scheme.

"I think they were looking for someone with a bit of pioneering spirit," she comments.

No-one was more surprised than Pease herself to be accepted. She had, in fact, aspirations to be a journalist and considered the training might give her a specialist edge as a reporter.

"I never thought I'd get it because a lot of the people who'd applied had been reading economics," she said. "But having got it, I thought I must take it."

Catching up on the maths training was inevitable, however. Pease felt that the other trainees were more numerate and took herself off to night-school to study accountancy. This gave her more of a handle on the subject matter. "As I got more useful and I learned a bit more, then I began to enjoy it," she says.

While this basic training obviously helped her career prospects, Pease found that enthusiasm went a long way too.

She explains: "In the first year, there was a three-month scheme where you got moved around. I did think that, at the end, everyone would say, "not having her!" but I tried to be friendly and open. And when I talked to someone on the international investment side and asked if they would consider taking me on, they did."

Being positive also helped Pease to reach the next step on the ladder. The investment department at Kleinwort at the time was small and Pease's immediate colleagues were very senior – meaning there was little time spare to train up a junior. Pease had previously met Basil Postan, who was then at Citibank. When he offered her a job, she moved across as a junior fund manager in European equities.

"I knew he'd be the most fantastic mentor and teacher and that's why I went there," she says.

Despite being descended from a family with connections to the City, Pease says that she had to make her own opportunities.

She says, "I didn't have a family saying 'hey, I'm going to introduce you to so-and-so' at all. There was no expectation for me to go to university, let alone to go into business. I can genuinely say that, on the way in, I don't think it gave me any opening at all."

In fact, Pease is doubtful that she would have been hired if she had been applying in today's environment.

She says, "It was a less global world then which meant there was less competition trying to get in. It still wasn't easy, but now I think it's really, really difficult."

This reflection has prompted Pease to turn her attention to the subject of recruitment in today's investment management industry. Numbers of applications have increased exponentially but the greater competition has actually made the selection process harder.

"How do you sift?" asks Pease. "We can't meet everybody. The criteria became increasingly focused on whether the candidate was at the LSE or Oxbridge or doing a very numerate degree subject."

The trend for the industry to hire very talented, but potentially identikit, graduates from a small pool of universities began to worry Pease.

Speaking to a friend, Andrew Formica (the Australian chief executive of Henderson Global Investors), she discovered she was not alone in her concerns. Formica was of the opinion that the investment groups had unintentionally "sleepwalked into narrowing the range".

"Andrew told me that he had looked at his existing fund managers and asked himself whether they looked anything like the Mr and Mrs Perfect who were coming in. The answer was that they didn't. And he said that really concerned him," Pease relates.

This sentiment chimed with Pease's own thinking as she believes attitude and aptitude to be as important as a degree.

"It's not all down to qualifications," she says. "You want someone with a great attitude, curiosity and reasonable people skills – and to give them a chance."

Formica had already initiated a project at Henderson to attract a broader spectrum of trainees. It was called Investment 2020 and Pease decided she wanted to get involved. With her own university education in literature, she was an ideal figurehead.

"If you are doing top-end derivatives, I'm sure it's incredibly useful to have a degree in maths or physics. But you don't need that for every job and we benefit from having different ways of thinking within a firm," she says.

Breaking into broking

Pease certainly needed to rely on skills other than her degree when faced with her first significant career challenge – building up a new European broking operation for Smith New Court.

"It was a challenge," she admits. "But if you try hard enough and ask people, you can learn it. It was really about getting a good enough group of people together and making it up as you go along."

Managing those people proved to be somewhat daunting initially.

She said: "I started in a room the size of a football pitch on my own and they were all traders; they'd come straight off the stock exchange floor. I found it tricky walking through in the morning. But, actually, once you gave a bit of humour back, it was fine."

Relations improved further as the business got off the ground.

"It wasn't a stuck-up sort of place. It was more like – 'if you can make money, if you can build something, then we'll give you respect,'" she adds.

As one of the early senior female participators in the City, Pease might have been a victim of sexual discrimination. In fact, her experience has been the opposite.

As a fund manager attending company visits, Pease often found herself sitting next to the most senior executive of the firm at the meeting.

Nowadays, Pease perceives there to be positive discrimination with women mostly being invited to take non-executive positions to increase the diversity of company boards – although this can be a double-edged sword.

She says, "You never want to be taken on just because you're female. You want to be taken on because you know you're going to be useful for the job. However, it makes companies more imaginative about giving people a break. The candidate might not have a picture-perfect CV but if they are a good thinker and they're going to bring something different to the job, then that's fine."

Pease could have been classed in that latter category when JO Hambro Capital Management was looking for a new chief executive.

After ten years at Smith New Court, she found she missed the stimulus of building out a business and was keen to take on that task at JO Hambro when the opportunity arose.

She was, however, pregnant with her third child. This may have been a cause for concern for some employers. Fortunately the board at JO Hambro was sufficiently visionary to hire her.

Pease says, "I had quite a good CV for the job I was going to. And so there was a trade – you're bringing some experience which the company doesn't have and you're gaining some flexibility."

With no staff and empty offices, Pease only needed to work three-day weeks to start, which quickly increased to full time as the business grew. She ensured she was organised enough to do the work in the time given and to be available when required.

"I was very aware," she says, "about how I did my work and that it wouldn't provide a bottleneck for anyone else because I wasn't there every day. I don't think it ever slowed the business up in any way."

Pease says she is grateful for the flexibility she enjoyed at JO Hambro. She believes that women can work and raise a family simultaneously – and it can be done most successfully on a case-by-case basis. Legislating for a blanket solution is not the answer, she maintained.

"There shouldn't be too much legislation dictating how firms work – particularly given most MPs haven't had commercial jobs," she argues. "I don't think they are in the best position to start dictating how commercial firms should work."

Pease says getting the balance of equity ownership right between fund managers and shareholders was her greatest test.

"I was always pro giving away quite a lot away because I felt the fund managers were adding the value and it was sensible to align their interests with the company's."

Pastoral care for the fund managers was another consideration. Being responsible for investing other people's money is a high-pressure job. Pease says, on occasion, psychoanalysts were brought in to help struggling managers.

She explains: "It's a lonely y business when it's going

wrong because, however much you lean out to somebody, ultimately they own that performance."

Support from colleagues, including herself as CEO, was vital in such circumstances. Most important of all was to contain any knee-jerk reactions and attempt to understand whether the underperformance was a short-term aberration or a longer-term trend.

Pease explains: "You can't have a panic every time a manager has a bad time and it's very important for the managers to feel that support."

Nonetheless, if a manager consistently underperforms, alternative action might have to be taken.

"Being a fund manager is a very well-paid job. If they really have lost their touch, you've got to be open and realistic about it."

Managing the managers can be a good deal easier if the right candidates are selected at the start. Pease says she got to know the personalities over time before offering any positions. Simply picking up the manager of the moment without doing any due diligence can be "quite a dangerous way of doing it."

She goes on: "The fund manager job gets the profile for investment management firms but, even if you include all the analysts and portfolio assistants, they're probably under 30% of the employees."

Therefore it is crucial that Investment 2020 focuses on attracting recruits to support functions as well as asset management itself. As a portal, Investment 2020 provides access to the firms but does not dictate where to place trainees. Pease is delighted to see that around 20% of placements have been in operations, around 12% in marketing, 12% in finance and just a little over that figure in risk.

She says: "All of these are important jobs with a serious career structure which is why we need a broad range of people coming through with different thinking."

So for those starting their careers now through Investment 2020, what does the will the industry look like in the future?

Pease foresees further advances in technology will help sift the "information overload" and make company research easier and more efficient. There could also be refinements in performance analysis. Pease devoted a great deal of her time at JO Hambro to watching fund managers and believes the system will move on from understanding market moves and style bias.

"There will be more focus on what's happening and why it's happening – what leads the manager to outperform or underperform, such as whether they are a good buyer or a good seller."

In a constantly changing world, how can an ambitious youngster equip themselves for a successful career in finance?

While economics degrees and MBAs appear to be a short cut to the top, other attributes can be as or more important. Enthusiasm is key to climbing the ladder, according to Pease. A new recruit should focus on learning, gaining skill-sets and trying to be as useful as possible.

"What employers don't want to see," she adds, "are recruits who quibble about the work or positions they are given."

Those who have achieved stellar academic success are particularly at risk from putting their own expectations ahead of the company's, she notes.

"The feedback from the employers involved in Investment 2020 has shown some common themes and lack of entitlement is very attractive," she says.

Opportunities arise from opportunities, she adds, explaining that luck can play a part but "good attitude" is a greater factor.

She concludes: "If you can get an opening in any of the 28 firms behind Investment 2020, you've got a great start – so make the most of it!"

What is Investment 2020?

A one-year recruitment programme for school-leavers and graduates, Investment 2020 aims to attract a wider pool of young and diverse talent to the investment management industry.

Nichola Pease, formerly CEO at JO Hambro and now a non-executive director at Schroders, helped launch the project in March 2013 and is now its chair.

By mid-2015, 28 firms had signed up and there were 550 trainees who were progressing through or had completed the programme.

The Investment 2020 website acts as an online hub where the participating companies can advertise trainee placements.

Once hired, the trainees earn a fair wage, guaranteed for the length of their contract, and will be awarded a certificate after the successful completion of 12 months.

As the trainees work within only one role, they build valid experience. There is the potential for them to be offered full time-employment after the contract finishes.

Additional training sessions, such as presentations by senior industry figures, and networking events are also on offer. This allows the recruits to make contacts within the investment industry.

Attracting school-leavers is a priority for Investment 2020. They are more difficult (and more expensive) to reach than graduates and the scheme can create some economies of scale for the investment firms.

Karis Stander, the managing director of Investment 2020, has introduced school visits to firms such as Henderson or Aberdeen as a way to raise awareness of both the industry and the trainee opportunities.

The message seems to have reached its target market as 40% of the trainees now joining Investment 2020 are school-leavers.

Pease comments: "Fund management is not like a bank with a big logo that everyone recognises. People don't really know what it's all about. We're trying to increase awareness by getting out and talking about what we do."

www.investment2020.org.uk

Conclusion

"Can you recommend a top fund manager?" is a question I've been asked countless times over the last two decades. I'm not authorised to give financial advice so would never recommended anyone, hence none of the fund managers interviewed here are people who manage money for either my retirement or on behalf of anyone in my family. But it's a question I can empathise with.

How do you identify a "top" manager from the thousands who operate in the sector? It is in many ways the $64,000 question and there is a whole industry that has grown up in the last 20 years dedicated to researching and rating fund managers which, while helping considerably, can also make the choice even harder for the private investor.

Hopefully, this book will shed some light on the less-talked about aspects of fund management. The secret, if there is one, is to do your research with the level of commitment and hard work that fund managers put into selecting companies to invest in.

They have patience – they invest for the long term, which means a minimum of five years; they do not trade or gamble, which means they are not making multiple investment decisions daily or weekly. Some of those interviewed hardly make a new investment decision more than once a year. Instead, they get to know the companies to ensure those companies continue to deliver returns.

They have humility – they recognise they are managing the retirement pots of ordinary people and that preserving wealth is, first and foremost, crucial. They accept their own limitations – they do not invest in areas or companies they do not understand. They stick to their own path and do not "follow the crowd".

They are passionate, inquisitive and challenging and, while they can be very clever, they keep it simple. They are not afraid to ask obvious questions about a company or question an investment consensus.

Above all, it's important to accept there is no archetypal fund manager – not all the interviewees have the same educational background or start in life. This not a career for a small elite, it is a career open to anyone who possesses the same traits as many of the fund managers appearing in this book, who are but a handful of those I have met over the years to have consistently made money for their investors.

And by buying this book you have made a small investment in the future of thousands of young people in the UK who need the help of the charities CHICKS and Place2Be, who are the main beneficiaries. Thank you.